D1526092

TenWorldPress

ALSO BY GLEN ALLISON
THE JOURNEY FROM KAMAKURA

PENIS GOURDS & MOSCOW MUGGINGS

A PHOTOGRAPHER'S TALES OF FAR-FLUNG TRAVELS

To Bob,
Never give up
your dreams!

[signature]

TEXT AND PHOTOGRAPHS **GLEN ALLISON**

PENIS GOURDS & MOSCOW MUGGINGS
A PHOTOGRAPHER'S TALES OF FAR-FLUNG TRAVELS
BY GLEN ALLISON

Published by:

TENWORLDPRESS

PO Box 641699
Los Angeles, CA 90064
Tel: 1-310-822-1534
Fax: 1-310-827-7198

Orders@TenWorldPress.com
http://www.TenWorldPress.com

FIRST EDITION

Publisher's Cataloging-in-Publication
(*Provided by Quality Books, Inc.*)
Allison, Glen, 1945-
Penis gourds & Moscow muggings : a photographer's tales of far-flung travels / by Glen Allison
p. cm.
ISBN 0-9719644-3-2
1. Allison, Glen, 1945---Journeys. 2. Photographers--United States--Biography. 3. Voyages and travels.
I. Title
TR140.A5535A3 2003   770'.92
QBI33-799

Library of Congress Control Number: 2002096024

Cover photo: Tribal Warrior, Irian Jaya, © 2002 Glen Allison
Edited by: Natalie Bates

ACKNOWLEDGMENTS

I would like to thank my inspirational friends: Giannis Agelou in Thessoloniki, Greece, as well as Larry Lee, Lou Jacobs Jr., Steve Cirillo and Jeff Hunter in California for their invaluable suggestions. Special thanks go to the tireless efforts of my publicist Antoinette Kuritz and my marketing consultant Carla Ruff. As usual, I am deeply indebted to my editor Natalie Bates for her diligent work and creative input. I am most appreciative of the invaluable contributions from Tina Rubin, my constant source of encouragement. I will never forget the help from my friend Annelie Cirillo in Munich, who offered me shelter and loaned me a thousand bucks when I was at rock bottom and stranded in Europe a decade ago—thanks for having trust in me. I offer appreciation to Janine Sang in New Zealand for encouraging me to write about my travel experiences. To Amnat Boonyeun in Bangkok, my deepest respect to you for your sincerity and your many translation efforts over the years. To Dominic in Papua New Guinea, thank you for sharing your soul and for safely guiding me through the jungles of the Sepik River. To Vuthi Seng in Phnom Penh, I can only hope to live up to your mission for world peace—the "killing fields" of past Cambodian history put your determination into perspective. And to my friend Sunil in Fiji, never give up your struggle. Your life depends on it.

Glen Allison

CONTENTS

1. GLOBAL PERSPECTIVE   1
2. THE JOURNEY BEGINS   4
3. UNITED STATES   8
4. EUROPE   13
5. VANUATU   20
6. IRIAN JAYA   24
7. PAPUA NEW GUINEA   31
8. RUSSIA   38
9. RED TAPE HASSLES   44
    PHOTOGRAPHS   55-86
10. THAILAND   87
11. VIETNAM   95
12. BALI   102
13. SULAWESI   112
14. CHINA   116
15. TURKEY   125
16. TIBET   129
17. TIMBUKTU   136
18. FINAL COMMENTS   146
    ABOUT THE AUTHOR   149

"A great human revolution in the life of a single individual has the power to change the destiny of a family, a society and the entire human race."

Daisaku Ikeda, September 8, 2002

1 GLOBAL PERSPECTIVE

This world is truly an exquisite place.

Too bad we haven't yet learned to celebrate the unique differences among ourselves. Wouldn't it be boring if we all had the same beliefs or the same color skin or ate the same food?

I wonder why it's so hard for us to melt the barriers we often find between ourselves—barriers that have existed for all eternity, it seems. I wonder at how we've allowed ourselves to become so narrow-minded and prejudiced. It can't be so impossible to learn the human heart.

I have one goal for my life—I want to build a bond with at least one person in every single country of the world before I die. Maybe trying to make more lifelong friendships, and nurturing those relationships, is all any of us can do.

Dr. Daisaku Ikeda, an acclaimed Buddhist peace advocate and the recipient of more than 130 honorary Ph.D.s from major universities of the world, had these words to say in his book *For the Sake of Peace*:

"Peace is not something to be left to others in distant places. It is something we create day to day in our efforts to cultivate care and consideration for others, forging bonds of friendship and trust in our respective communities through our own actions and example."

He goes on to say, "The problems confronting

humankind are daunting in their depth and complexity. While it may be hard to see where to begin—or how—we must never give in to cynicism or paralysis. We must each initiate action in the direction we believe to be right. We must refuse the temptation to passively accommodate ourselves to present realities and embark upon the challenge of creating a new reality. In addition to these efforts in the public sphere, it is equally essential to create in concrete, tangible ways a culture of peace in daily life."

Unfortunately, it seems that all too often we human beings have chosen to take advantage of each other. Maybe our philosophical beliefs haven't been forged deep enough; perhaps the will to coexist and to revere all life isn't yet that strong.

But I remain optimistic.

The truth of the matter is that in everyday life it's often hard to live up to such lofty ideals. I know this all too well. Many of the experiences I relate in this book were a bit painful to endure. So many times all I could do was sit back and laugh at the insane circumstances in which I found myself ensnared. I was forced to take a good hard look at myself, trying to discover the same frailties in my own life that I so often saw in the actions of those who might have perpetrated injustice against me. Often there was no other choice but to look at life through a new lens.

I've wondered from time to time why I came into contact with so many unusual characters in my travels. But, on reflection, I know exactly why my path crossed theirs, if only for a brief moment. I needed to learn something about myself, or about humankind.

Laughing about the quirkiness of it all has enabled the lessons to be that much more poignantly learned, even though sometimes the humor could only be found in retrospect.

In the following pages I'll poke fun at some of the crazy predicaments I've encountered, with the intention of illustrating how diverse are the ways human beings have chosen to relate with one another—for better or worse—and the lessons that can be learned.

In the last paragraph of *For the Sake of Peace* Dr. Ikeda concluded, "The human spirit is endowed with the ability to transform even the most difficult circumstances, creating value and ever richer meaning. When each person brings this limitless spiritual capacity to full flower, and when ordinary citizens unite in a commitment to positive change, a culture of peace—a century of life—will come into being."

2 THE JOURNEY BEGINS

Before we start this marathon excursion, perhaps I should explain what led me to forsake all my worldly possessions (at age 45) and to commence what turned out to be a *very* long trip—eight years continuously roaming the globe with no permanent place to live, during which I photographed 131 countries and territories. Along the way I visited some of the "strangest" places on this planet. Maybe I was the first international homeless person, I don't know.

In the ensuing pages I'll share my "secret" hints for safely traveling the world with costly professional photo gear, plus a few guidelines about fighting off muggers in Moscow. I'll offer tips on how to avoid being burned at the stake by penis-gourd-clad tribal warriors while trekking deep within the leech-infested jungles of Irian Jaya—info many travelers might need to know. I tell my story in the context of what most people might say is a *very* unusual way to live. Though many have suggested (like my mother, for example) that I should get a "real" job, I beg to differ with them on that point, as you might agree when you've finished reading this book.

So why did I choose to live such a strange life?

It all began in 1990 under the most inauspicious circumstances imaginable—at least to me. I started living my dream by delivering pizzas. The financial recession that year caused a massive drop in the value of Southern California real estate in which I was heavily invested at the time. In short order I was forced into a devastating bankruptcy.

There I was, penniless, living in my van and delivering pizzas in Los Angeles.

My bankruptcy put the final brush strokes on what had been a flourishing career as an architectural photographer—a career I eventually had grown tired of. My dream was to shoot travel images. So I did what any self-respecting professional photographer would surely have done at such a juncture—I destroyed the previous twenty years of architectural negatives in my file, the entire body of my life's work!

Yes, my peers said I was *crazy*.

Many thought I had indeed finally gone mad. Photographers don't destroy their negatives—they guard them with all their might. Those negatives were all I had to show for years of struggle. Years exerted to carve out my little place in this world. Photographers' souls are embodied in their pictures, and those pictures are important to their posterity. After all, the moment photographers click the shutter they own the copyrights to their images for seventy years after they die, according to current U.S. copyright law. My friends begged and pleaded with me not to destroy my heritage. Surely I would regain my senses soon.

But I refused to listen.

I went to my computer and methodically deleted every single client's name, telephone number and address. Determined never to look back, I decided to burn all the bridges behind me. Finally I was free from the constraints of my past—superficially at least.

Now I could make a fresh start.

I should add that while I might have been somewhat destitute at that particular moment, for the previous two decades I'd led a rather illustrious life as one of the most sought-after architectural photographers in the United States. During the three years prior to my bankruptcy I earned one million dollars. I lectured extensively, speaking at universities and major photo conferences around the country. I conducted photo workshops to national parks and had my travel appetite whetted by lecturing on complementary cruises to Alaska and the Mediterranean for Princess and Royal Viking Cruise Lines, an appetite that became a craving when I led photo workshops for UCLA to the enchanting isles of Tahiti, Moorea and Bora Bora. Up to that point my photographs had been published in excess of 5000 times on the covers and pages of the most prestigious architectural magazines in the world. It seemed as though photographers from around the globe wanted to learn the secrets to my success. The very day I threw all my negatives into the trash bin (actually I gave them back to the clients, not keeping even one single negative for myself), *Architectural Digest* called to offer me an assignment for their next issue. Naturally I did what any "former" world-renowned architectural photographer would have done: I declined the assignment. I simply told them that I did *not* do that kind of photography anymore. Thank you very much.

Though I was at rock bottom, I decided to make changes in my life, to do something new—even if I had to swallow my pride and keep delivering pizzas for a while. My biggest fear was that I would inadvertently wind up delivering a pizza to one of my former architectural clients and then have to pretend that I owned that pizza shop and that my delivery boy was out sick for the evening.

I found myself without a dime in my pocket and no roof over my head, except for the van I was living in. But in my heart I knew I was finally free to be a travel photographer, who could roam the globe at will. My lifelong goal would come to fruition. There was absolutely no doubt in my mind; I was convinced of my future success.

Little did I know what was in store for me.

Okay, okay. I know all you avid travelers are yearning to get this trip on the road and all the photographers out there have been eagerly awaiting my first photo tip.

Well . . . I've already given it to you.

We must find a way to follow our dreams.

3 UNITED STATES

In case you're wondering how I started financing my world travels so soon after a bankruptcy, it wasn't easy. In fact it seemed almost impossible in the beginning. Over the years I've tried to block my memory of the day, back in 1990, that I filed for bankruptcy in the Los Angeles Superior Court. Today my recollection of that experience has become one of my golden treasures in life, but back then it was very disheartening.

As relayed in the pages of this book, we will soon embark on a tour to some of the most exotic locales on this earth. To date my pictures of these destinations have been published more than 50,000 times. However, I must admit that it was rough going in the beginning. Sometimes it looked impossible. But somehow I was motivated to never give up.

I discovered that the official date of my bankruptcy would put my financial obligations on hold for nine months, during which time the law couldn't touch my assets, nor would I need to make any payments on my debts. At a massive garage sale I sold my expensive leather furniture, marble tables, *objets d'art* and almost everything else I owned—except my cameras. Then I rented out my half-million dollar house to a British rock group, who were in L.A. to record a new album. Planning to live on the monthly income for the next nine months, I headed off to photograph the United States and Canada—at least for the nine months before the bankruptcy became final when I would lose the house and my van too.

Luckily, based on a handful of travel images from past journeys, I was offered a contract from one of the world's premier stock photo libraries, Tony Stone Images in London. Nowadays the agency is simply known as "Stone" and has long since been gobbled up by the Getty Images' empire. Though I'd found a place to sell my soon-to-be-photographed travel pictures, I needed to find a way to finance my trips and to pay for the shooting expenses I'd incur. Perhaps all I should say is that I was "very creative" in that endeavor. Though I had lost everything else I owned, I'd figured out a way to keep my camera equipment. I won't say how.

Eventually I made my way to New York and to the Statue of Liberty. More precisely, I was in New Jersey looking at the statue with the New York skyline in the background. I'd seen a previous photo taken from that point of view—a telephoto image of the statue with it's torch perfectly framed between the two World Trade Center towers. It was important to shoot my picture in a significantly different way. (Regrettably, that photo is now historical.)

Eventually I found the position where the other photographer must have stood. Apparently he'd placed his tripod halfway out on a narrow pier that extended into the Hudson River. However, the middle of the pier was now missing! You couldn't walk out far enough so that the torch could be positioned dead center between the two towers, the most logical placement.

Fair enough, I chuckled. The other shooter must have destroyed that section of the pier as soon as he finished his picture. Now no one could ever take the same image from that exact spot again.

To insure my photo would be very different, I needed to find my own unique vantage point anyway. I carried on with my search. Eventually I found the perfect position: it was inside a huge boat yard several miles from the first location. An immense sign read, "NO TRESPASSING, VIOLATORS WILL BE PROSECUTED AND/OR SHOT OR EATEN."

Since there didn't seem to be a guard on duty and I couldn't see any hungry dogs lounging about, I drove through the open gate, and I soon found the perfect position from which to shoot my "prize-winning" photo. But the weather was extremely hazy that night. It was a good five miles from me to Miss Liberty and even farther to the New York skyline. My picture would have Lady Liberty's torch exactly centered between the two World Trade Center towers but the image, when magnified by a 600mm telephoto lens, looked like mush in my viewfinder. Giving up, I collapsed my tripod and escaped from the premises undetected.

The next evening the sky was incredibly clear and most likely I would never get another chance to shoot that picture with no haze, so I headed back to the same maritime yard. Only this time the gate was sealed shut. An irritable-looking guard sat in the guardhouse. A huge gun was strapped to his exuberant waistline. And by the look on the man's face, I was pretty certain he would *not* be opening the gate for me that night.

Not wanting to forfeit what would probably be an

incredible photo, I donned my most enthusiastic smile and with bubbly effervescence described to the guard the picture I wanted to shoot. Surprisingly, he lifted a very greasy hand from the giant pizza on his lap and pushed a button, causing the gate to swing open. "Help yourself, Buddy," he bellowed.

For the next ten years I made huge sales on that photo (it's the first picture in my collection in the center section of this book, page 55) and I'm glad I didn't kow-tow to my anxiety that night. This lesson has enabled me to shoot many high-earning images from some very unlikely vantage points. Many of those experiences were rather risky, even hair-raising, like the night I was caught on the rooftop of a defense building in Bangkok smack in the middle of a Thai military coup. Machine guns surrounded me. But that's another story, which you will soon read.

Knowing I'd taken a successful shot of Miss Liberty's profile that night, I headed back into Jersey to find a good place to sleep. I was pinching pennies (you remember, of course, that I was facing imminent bankruptcy) and prepared myself for another night in the van. For safety I would always find a brightly lit parking lot next to an expensive hotel. Up ahead was a Holiday Inn. It was too expensive for me, so I figured its parking lot would be just fine.

It was a stiflingly hot and humid night on the East Coast in July. I feared leaving my windows open more than a half inch in case a robber or gang member might find what they considered easy prey. My clothes soon became drenched in sweat; it was almost too hot to breathe inside my van. As each hour passed another layer of my clothing came off till eventually I was sleeping *au naturel*. I awoke when a powerful searchlight began sweeping the interior of my van and someone shouted, "He's buck-naked in there!"

Jolted awake, I knew at any minute I'd be robbed and knifed by a gang member, or maybe even raped by some pervert. Turns out, it was the police! This was going to be real hard to tell my mom back in Los Angeles when I would have to call and have her wire money to bail me out of jail.

In the heat of the night I'd apparently been having an erotic dream. At that particular moment all I could find was a loose sock to cover my modesty. (I hadn't yet been to Irian Jaya and didn't have one of those giant gourds handy like the one on the cover of this book.) Fortunately things quickly settled down. After hearing my "bankruptcy sob story" the cops only reprimanded me and let me go—though they did ask that I put some clothes on.

I drove around Jersey the rest of that night till I found a twenty-four-hour diner where I filled my stomach with the blackest coffee they had. Crouched in a lone corner booth, I pondered my destiny till dawn.

4 EUROPE

After nine months I had zigzagged across forty-eight states and had visited all the major cities in Canada. My van's odometer registered an additional seventy-five thousand miles on the day I returned to Los Angeles, which was just in the nick of time to drop the vehicle off at the bank a couple of hours before the bankruptcy became final.

I'd taken thousands of pictures, and my new agency had accepted many. But having images accepted and having them sold were two different things, I discovered. I was to get fifty-percent royalties from all sales, but fifty percent of nothing wasn't very much. In fact, I had received some money from the agency a few weeks back—$770 for almost a year's work. Not bad, I thought, trying to put a spin on the situation. It was imperative to keep a positive attitude, but things weren't adding up, as I could see it.

By then I had lost the van and the income from my house—the bank now owned them both. Carefully evaluating the situation, it was obvious I needed a nice little trip to Europe to get my mind off my financial disaster.

After discovering I had enough leftover air miles for a free roundtrip ticket, I sold my giant 600mm-f/4 lens for $5000. It was too big to lug along on the trip anyway. With the newfound cash I bought a large bag of film and a six-month Eurail pass, leaving only a few hundred dollars in my pocket. I wouldn't worry about running out of cash in Europe until it happened. Well . . . it did happen, more than a couple of times. A few weeks later I tried to keep a stiff upper lip when I found myself on the streets of Amsterdam panhandling for food. Taking my cameras to a Dutch pawnshop was the last thing I wanted to do. Those cameras were my only tangible lifeline to hope for the future. I couldn't lose them, too.

Despite the challenge, I persevered.

There wasn't a famous icon in Europe that escaped my lens—Dutch windmills, Big Ben, the Matterhorn, Oktoberfest and the sleek gondolas of Venice—only to mention a handful. I backpacked across Europe for six months, staying at a different youth hostel almost every night if I had the money to spare, but usually I slept in a seat on an overnight train to the next city since the Eurail pass was already paid for.

In Rome I learned a good lesson from an extremely skillful petty thief.

Train stations in Italy are notorious for pickpockets and purse-snatchers, who relieve you of your valuables in the most ingenious ways. I must hand it to them for that. One day I was walking across the parking lot in front of the Rome train station—not something a wise person would do in the height of the tourist season, especially if he or she were carrying ten thousand dollars worth of camera equipment as I was. Seemingly out of nowhere a crowd of about twenty people appeared. Several passersby "accidentally" bumped into me. Well,

I'm no dummy and I knew exactly what was going on. I held my cameras and tripod tightly against my body. My wallet had already been stuffed deeply into the front button-down pocket of my snug trousers. If someone had even tried to get his hand in there, I would have known it.

I plowed through the crowd seemingly unscathed and kept walking, all the while making sure nothing was missing. About a block farther ahead a passing Italian called my attention to my backside. Reaching behind, I discovered that someone in the crowd must have spilled a thick, creamy substance all over my shirt and the back of my trousers. Naturally I became extremely wary of everything and everyone around me.

I walked another block until I found a safe place to dismount my gear and to remove the gunk off my rear. I made sure my camera bag and tripod were leaning against my legs so I'd know if someone tried to take them. Several "friendly" Italians tried their best to distract me, but I completely ignored them until someone started screaming so loudly I had to look up from my gooey task. The guy was going totally ballistic, frantically pointing in a direction behind me. He probably was working in cahoots with some pickpocket hiding behind a nearby bush, who would grab my stuff as soon as my head was turned. The man persisted to such an extent that I finally looked over my shoulder. To my horror I saw my camera bag running down the street in the hands of a thief.

No way could I lose my cameras; not after all I'd been through. Besides, my photo gear was all I had left in the world. Tripod raised high, I gave chase with a rush of adrenaline—and a definite intent to kill, planning to use my tripod as the lethal weapon. The thief turned to see if I was behind him. Maybe he felt my steaming breath on his neck, or maybe he figured he had very little time left on this Earth.

The fury in my eyes must have left no doubt in his mind that he was about to die. So he dropped my camera bag and kept running. I, of course, abruptly ended my chase, and the murderous intent gushing through my veins rapidly dissipated.

Another lesson well learned: Now whenever I put my bags down, without fail I always place my feet inside the shoulder straps. No one will take my cameras again without dragging me along too.

It was time to leave Italy so I jumped on the next train to Milano and from there immediately boarded the midnight special to Barcelona.

I'd received a couple of small checks from my agency. Even so, there were only a few dollars in my pocket. My sister, who was taking care of my "financial" affairs back home, had deposited those checks into my bank account in L.A. Every few days I used my ATM card to retrieve cash. I had a hundred bucks left in the bank so my situation wasn't desperate yet. Upon arrival in Barcelona I popped my ATM card in the first machine I saw and withdrew fifty dollars in pesetas. I'd lost all my credit cards in the bankruptcy, including my Platinum American Express card. The only plastic in my wallet was a check card with a Plus symbol on the back which enabled me to withdraw cash from any ATM machine with a like symbol displayed—if there was any money in my account.

Not wanting to squander cash on a youth hostel, after a day of heavy shooting in Barcelona I boarded another night train, this time to France.

Paris is an expensive city, so my meager funds disappeared fast. While trying to find an ATM machine with a Plus symbol, I soon discovered I was out of luck, which shocked me. Today, of course, France does have those Plus symbols on their ATMs, but they didn't in the early '90s. With only ten dollars in my pocket, I called my sister collect in California and was pleasantly surprised—ecstatic, I should say—to learn the latest check from my agency was for $5000. Since there was never much of a balance in my account, the bank had placed a one-week hold on the funds.

With only ten dollars to last a week, it was time to leave Paris and catch a night train to Munich, where I kept my things stored at a friend's place. Surely Germany had those Plus symbols so I could at least withdraw the remaining fifty dollars from my account.

But when I arrived in Munich the next morning, much to my dismay Germany didn't seem to have those Plus symbols either. After mooching some food at my friend's place, and with only five dollars to my name, more panhandling on the street would be necessary unless she was told what was going on. But I was too embarrassed. That night I boarded another night train back to Milano, thinking surely Italy had those Plus symbols.

But Italy didn't have them either.

Now just two dollars were in my pocket.

The only alternative was to buy a small bottle of water and a piece of bread with the remaining cash, then board another night train to Barcelona, where I knew exactly where to find an ATM machine with a Plus symbol. My Eurail pass entitled me to unlimited travel.

I decided not to complain. Back in the '70s I had started practicing Buddhism, which back then was a "very cool" California thing to do. So I fully understood it was important not to make my bad karma worse by complaining or manifesting a negative attitude. Why dig my hole any deeper? My situation was distressing enough as it was. But, hey, how many people would have given a left arm to be traveling around Europe footloose and fancy free like me? I tried to convince myself. My stomach, clenched on nothing but stomach acid, growled in response.

Four hours later the train came to an abrupt halt at the French border. The French were having one of their famous train strikes. There was no way I'd be in Barcelona the next morning, and there was no alternative but to hang out at the last Italian train station till the next night train left for Munich, where I knew there would at least be a warm meal and a hot shower at my friend's place. After my arrival, desperate, I called my sister to see if she could wire me some money. She suggested I simply go back to the last ATM I'd visited and get some cash. She'd never been to Europe. I explained that going to that particular ATM machine was like taking the train from Los Angeles to New York.

When I arrived at my friend's apartment in Munich, she thought I'd gone totally insane. Swallowing my pride, I finally told her the reason for my hasty return. In a flash she went to her bank and came home with a thousand dollars to loan me. It was raining in Munich at the time. To say the least, my work had been

GLEN ALLISON

extremely unproductive during the previous week with all those train rides. The weather was nice in Italy just a few hours ago. That evening I boarded my seventh night train in a row and went straight back to Milano.

After that experience, my agency's sales skyrocketed and I never ran out of money again. Perhaps the Universe had been testing me, but capitulated on seeing the strength of my resolve to never give up.

5 VANUATU

After my return to Los Angeles, I was without a car or a place to live, though now it was by choice since the royalties from my agency were starting to roll in. Not having roots had begun to grow on me. The monthly checks from my agency had increased dramatically. Even so, I conserved funds by staying at the inexpensive Half Moon Motel in West L.A. One week after my arrival I was on a flight to Tahiti, the start of my first around-the-world trip.

Hop-scotching my way across the South Pacific, I visited twenty-five exotic islands, eventually finding myself in Vanuatu on the remote coral-reefed island of Tanna—home of one the world's most accessible active volcanoes, mighty Mount Yasur.

Dozens of pigs and chickens scattered as my tiny, chartered plane landed on the grass airstrip. When I climbed out, there was an eerie sense of foreboding in the air. In the distance Mount Yasur grumbled and snarled, then disgorged black streams of smoke into the late afternoon sky. It might be dangerous up there, but I'd never stood on the rim of a spewing volcano before. I climbed into a waiting Jeep. The driver fired up the engine and headed off toward Mount Yasur. Off to one side were several curious onlookers shaking their heads in disbelief.

Maybe they knew something I didn't.

For the first ten miles we plowed through a dense jungle. It was almost impossible to see daylight above the narrow, chiseled slit of a path that had been hacked through the tropical ferns. Eventually we found ourselves on a black, desert moonscape of volcanic ash. Up and around the backside of Yasur's throbbing mid-section we drove until the Jeep could go no farther.

The driver brought the vehicle to a grinding halt, powdered black dust swirling round our heads. His expression seemed to indicate that I was outrageously stupid for wanting to go up to the crater's rim alone.

He couldn't be convinced to join me.

Yasur had been quiet for some time. I hoped the volcano wasn't just holding its breath, conserving its energy and getting ready to blow the whole mountain to Mars!

When I reached the top, an ominous sound pulled at me. I crept to the rim of the crater and fearfully peeked over the edge to see what was inside. There, leering before me, five hundred feet directly below, was a fire-scorched furnace of red-hot bristling vents ready to blow at any second. Turgid. Revengeful—a soot-filled dungeon of spewing lava.

The primal forces of nature—the danger that surrounded me—was frightening. Was this madness? Why had I come here? Why was I so enamored of Yasur's seductive pull?

My face tensed.

It wasn't safe here.

Yasur spat more flames, an evil tongue of fire licking at me. The volcano was ready to devour whatever creature strayed too close to the edge. I knew it was always quietest before the storm. What was Yasur waiting for?

Ominously, the fuming volcano remained calm, so I quickly set up my tripod, then used the toe of my hiking boot to gingerly test the edge of the crater. The ground seemed firm. It seemed safe.

More fear tugged at my shirtsleeve.

It was almost dark. I had hoped to shoot at twilight—hot, fiery lava glowing in the night sky. Suddenly, Yasur roared with an explosion almost loud enough to burst my eardrums. The wind concussion was so violent that the suck of air nearly pulled me over the edge.

I grabbed my tripod and held it steady.

When I looked up, lava was bursting in midair like Fourth-of-July fireworks, an amazing pyrotechnic display with luminous strands of fire blasting through the sky. (See my photo # 856263-002 at http://www.gettyimages.com.) After shooting several frames, I paused for a moment, waiting for Yasur's next angry expletive. I didn't have to wait long—Yasur was alive!

Each fireworks display of flaming, molten lava rose five hundred feet into the sky until reaching its terminal velocity. The lava hung weightlessly for a second then started falling back toward earth.

Toward me!

Dodging the flying, red-hot streams of fire, I ducked fast to escape a passing two thousand-degree clump of molten lava, which landed about fifteen feet behind me. Gasping for breath in the rising sulfuric fumes, I frantically nailed a couple more shots. Surely photographers must be either possessed or crazy. It was time to run for my life! Snapping the quick-release to free my camera, I grabbed the tripod and jumped swiftly to one side, trying to avoid more midair volcanic debris. But I lost my footing, slipping on some gravel, and my tripod careened over the edge of the crater.

Lying flat on my stomach, legs spread, toes digging in, I gasped for breath in the sulfur-tainted air and frantically stretched head-first over the edge of the crater's lip, struggling to grab the tripod before it slipped farther down the treacherous slope and out of reach. The fiery conflagration stared straight into my eyes. My tripod's awkward shape kept it from slipping farther down.

The volcano pulled at me; my face was drenched in cold sweat. I held onto the tripod with one hand and dug the fingers of my other hand into the crater wall, desperately trying to get a handhold before my body slipped over the edge.

Yasur grumbled and snarled—

The harder I pulled at the tripod, the more the incline caved away. Finally, I yanked the tripod over the edge and to safety just as the volcano violently exploded with an ear-shattering roar.

Grabbing my camera bag, I dashed away as the molten inferno gurgled and spat in hateful revenge.

Seeing me charging downhill, my driver revved up the engine. I dove into the back of the Jeep as it lurched forward and sped away, wheels spinning black plumes of volcanic ash back into Yasur's face. Swerving and fishtailing, we flew down the mountain.

That's the last volcano I'll ever shoot.

6 IRIAN JAYA

Irian Jaya is the easternmost province of Indonesia, located adjacent to Papua New Guinea, about a thousand kilometers due north of Darwin, Australia. Only fifty or sixty years ago there were people living in Irian Jaya who had yet to be discovered by the Civilized White Man. The Irian culture was as pagan then as it had been for five thousand years. Even as recently as ten or fifteen years ago there were reported cases of cannibalism. Eating one's enemy enabled the victor to absorb the loser's qualities of valor and bravery. Perhaps more important, it was the foremost insult.

I must tell you now that what happened to me in that remote wilderness will seem unbelievable. But this story is based on actual events, as are all the episodes in this book.

My plane landed in Jayapura, the Irian capital, and from there I flew to the town of Wamena in the heart of the Baliem Valley. As the little twelve-seater plane banked its wings on final approach toward the landing strip, I caught sight of a dozen men emerging from the surrounding bush, all excitedly pointing at our plane. I'd seen pictures of the Dani villagers in magazines and guidebooks, but it was a curious sight seeing them in real life—naked except for the huge gourds they wore on their penises and which were now standing at full attention. I couldn't help wondering how they kept their gourds so erect—I doubted whether they'd somehow discovered the modern wonders of Viagra.

When the plane taxied to a stop, several inquisitive Dani tribesmen gathered nearby as the passengers disembarked, then they followed us to our waiting jeeps parked at the edge of the grass landing strip. Their gourds cast immense shadows in the bright afternoon sunlight, and I couldn't help thinking that their "excitement" made them look as though it might be their first day at a nudist colony. Though a bit disconcerting, I assumed I'd get used to having so many upright gourds following me all day. Without looking closely it was impossible to determine how they kept those things pointing straight up.

We were driven to a nearby hotel from which we'd be departing early the next morning on a trek deep into the far reaches of the Baliem Valley.

The first day of my trek would take me to a remote village where I'd be spending the night with the locals. I'd hired a Dani tribesman to carry my gear. With all due respect to his native attire—or lack thereof—I still chuckled at the sight: A naked man wearing a penis gourd on one side and my backpack on the other. Still trying not to scrutinize the situation too closely, I kept wondering how his gourd stayed attached as he leaped across streams from boulder to boulder.

I'd been burning off insidious leeches all day. Blood oozed down my legs. My body ached with exhaustion and I was drenched in sweat. The insufferable humidity caused my glasses to fog, making it almost impossible for me to see through my camera's viewfinder. Thank goodness for auto-focus lenses.

Suddenly to the left, the jungle ferns rustled.

Before I knew it, I was completely surrounded by a dozen tribal warriors, their spears and poison blow darts at the ready. There was no time to make a run for it; a vicious savage grabbed me from behind. Kicking and screaming, I was dragged to a nearby village where men danced around a raging bonfire.

Honest, this is true.

The ugliest, most unsympathetic warrior—the one with the largest bone in his nose and the most impressive, most sharply pointed gourd I'd ever seen—hoisted me above his shoulders and began parading me around the fire.

Oh, my God! This must be the end, I thought.

Surely I wouldn't be burned at the stake, but I was more scared the guy might drop me. I didn't want my mom getting a letter from the Indonesian government, "Dear Mrs. Allison, we regret to inform you that your son was killed when he was speared in the rear by a gigantic penis gourd."

She just wouldn't understand.

Off to one side my guide was laughing his head off. He'd known all along that my tour had included a mock capture in the jungle. I soon discovered that most tourists who go to Irian Jaya receive such thrills.

Later that day several "warriors" speared a little pig, skinned him, wrapped him in banana leaves, and then cooked him in an earth-oven under sizzling, red-hot stones. At least it wasn't me rolled up in those leaves. Finally I relaxed, but I wished I had a stiff shot of whisky in my hand. I hadn't brought any, of course.

Just like I hadn't brought any Scotch brand # 202 super-stick masking tape either, which I surely wished I had after looking inside my camera bag.

When traveling, I always remove my film from the yellow (or green) boxes and out of the little plastic containers. To conserve space, the film leaders get taped to the cassettes with masking tape just to keep everything tidy. But no, this time I had decided to save a few pennies by buying a cheaper brand of masking tape. With the intense humidity, the leaders on three hundred rolls of film had come loose. It looked like spaghetti inside my camera bag. Never again will I leave home without super-adhesive Scotch brand # 202!

Later that evening everyone gathered round the campfire and finally I had a chance to observe how those penis gourds were rigged. At least my curiosity was satisfied. Not only was there a tiny hole drilled through the tip of the gourd through which passed an almost invisible string that looped around their upper abdomens, another tiny hole was drilled at the bottom, tied with a string cinched tightly around their exposed testicles.

So it was simple physics, not arousal, that kept their gourds up all day.

As guest of honor, I was invited by the village chief to sleep over that night. One of his many wives let me sleep in her bed—by myself, of course. Fortunately I'd brought along my compact silk sleeping sheet, which was conveniently stored in its own little pouch.

The bed had a raised wooden frame with a recessed mattress inside. The men may wear humongous gourds, but in reality the Irian people are very small in stature. That bed was tiny; I had to sleep in a tight fetal position.

Sleep!

I never slept.

Rats! Dozens scurried across the rafters all night long. With each passing hour they grew more venturesome and playful. Several began running circles around my bed frame. Fearing for my life, I grabbed my miniature high-intensity flashlight, which I never leave at home. If I could at least see those rats, maybe I could fight them off. There must have been a point when sleep came—or maybe what happened next was real, I don't know—but I assume I was dreaming when a giant rat started dragging me off the bed!

I awoke, screaming at the top of my lungs.

The village chief came running—spear in hand but sans gourd—to see what was the matter. I kept raving at the top of my lungs, perhaps more in fear of the chief than the rats. I vowed not to forget to bring a bottle of Valium on my next trip—and maybe a few mouse traps too.

The next morning I was up *very* early, more than ready to hit the trail.

My guide and I trudged through the jungle for several hours toward the next village. Soon we heard drums announcing our imminent arrival. When we approached the village, we saw that several tribes' people had already laid their wares along the path in hopes I might want to buy a few souvenirs. The women carried bilum bags that were woven with a net type structure. One end of the bag narrowed to a "handle," which they strapped over their heads, slinging the bag over their back. They put sweet potatoes or taro root inside. Several carried babies that way too. Included in their wares were intricately hand-woven baskets, wood-carved idols and several voodoo dolls. I considered buying one of those dolls for a former architectural client I never liked very much and a bilum bag for my mom. But upon closer inspection, it was obvious that the bags were used ones; the "handles" were matted and soiled. Obviously the women had just pulled them off their heads as they rushed from the fields hoping I might want to purchase some gifts. At the end of the display there were a couple of really *huge* penis gourds.

What a great gift for myself!

I picked up the larger of the two gourds thinking the size seemed appropriate. Then I realized that these gourds might not be new either after noticing the one I held was still warm.

I dropped it to the ground rather quickly.

Perhaps the most important lesson to learn in Irian Jaya is to never ask for small change. In the not too distant past the Irians' unit of monetary currency was the pig. With pigs the men could buy food, land or even wives. (It's a male-dominated society down there.) Then the Indonesian government introduced hard currency: coins and bills. But the men of Irian Jaya don't have any pockets—only gourds!

Another note of interest, when Europeans count using their fingers, they usually raise the thumb to indicate the number "one." Americans on the other hand, usually raise the index finger to indicate the same number. Naturally in most societies when all the fingers on one hand are raised, this signifies the number "five." But not in Irian Jaya. They simply raise a clinched fist when they want five of something. Traditionally it seems that older women would chop off a digit of a finger every time a loved one died. After enough relatives had passed on, they no longer had five fingers to raise, so lifting a clinched fist became the norm.

On the day I left the country, I happened across a curio shop on the way to the airport. Inside I found dozens of voodoo dolls, piles of snakeskin drums and a big stack of funeral masks. And displayed on one wall were at least two hundred penis gourds of every size and configuration imaginable.

Temptation seized me!

Taking a chance that the gourds weren't the "previously owned" models, I excitedly asked the sales clerk if there was a fitting room.

7 PAPUA NEW GUINEA

From Jayapura I flew to Australia and eventually ended up in Darwin, a rather provincial outpost that has always served as a refuge for those escaping the monsoon rains of summer and the hungry crocodiles, which are there all year long.

There's a restaurant in Darwin called "The Hard Croc Café."

Those penis gourd adventures in Irian Jaya had opened my eyes to the excitement of jungle travel and now I was ready for more. Papua New Guinea wasn't far away, so I prepared my things. I'd heard that a trip to PNG would be much more dangerous that my sojourn to visit the Irians, and I definitely didn't want to take my exposed film along. As it was, I feared for my life and didn't want to take a chance on sacrificing my film to the gods too. But I couldn't find a professional color lab to process my film in Darwin. So I drove around till I spotted a commercial portrait studio. I stopped, introduced myself to the owner, and asked where he had his film processed. It turns out there was a "really sensitive" guy who worked at the one-hour place down the street. The kid had built a good reputation by catering to the pro shooters in town—a handful at most. An hour later after happily editing my perfectly processed film, I express-mailed it to my agency just minutes before the next flight to my much-feared destination.

It was a hard decision to dispose of the huge gourd I'd been carrying for the last couple of weeks. To make matters worse, it was shaped like a giant corkscrew. It wouldn't even fit into my backpack. Okay, I must admit, I *had* "modeled" it in front of the mirror a couple of times and concluded that my profile didn't look all that bad. At least I'd finally been able to rid myself of gourd envy. Reluctantly, I made the decision to toss the thing in the trash. Who'd buy my well-used gourd anyway?

Once in Papua New Guinea, I chartered yet another tiny plane to fly me north to the Sepik River, which is like the Amazon of PNG, only much smaller. I boarded a motorized dugout canoe and headed upstream deep into PNG's darkest jungles. My guide warned me not to keep dragging my hands in the Sepik's warm waters lest my fingers become lunch for starving piranhas.

Crocodiles, on the other hand, play an important role in local society. Even today, the men of the Sepik sport body carvings that make their skin resemble that of a crocodile. The effect is created by slashing several hundred inch-long cuts in their skin, front and rear, into which they pack fresh mud. That makes the wounds heal in scarred, raised welts, causing their skin to have a permanent crocodile like engraved pattern. Clean mud is packed into the cuts, not only to stem infection, but to cause the welts to be more defined when they heal.

We stopped at a riverside village about a week after one of those crocodile-cutting ceremonies had occurred. These events last three weeks, during which the youthful male participants heal from their cuts. All the bloodletting occurs on the first day. The young men wear only a clump of wild reeds dangling from their waist to cover their private parts in front. For three weeks they are secluded in the village spirit house away from the women and children. With their bodies covered in cuts on both sides, they can't lie down for almost a month because of the painful healing process. Instead, when they try to sleep, they stand and hang their chins over a horizontal bamboo pole.

This cutting ceremony is their right of passage from youth to adulthood. I didn't ask if they practiced circumcision or if their crocodile patterns covered everything. The more I thought about it, maybe penis gourds weren't such a bad idea after all.

After a week on the Sepik, I reboarded my tiny, chartered aircraft and headed to the Huli Highlands. My guide warned me that the area was quite dangerous at times. The local tribes were famous for their continuous clan warfare, but he told me if we encountered such battles the warriors would most likely let us pass unharmed—they were only interested in killing each other.

This fact didn't reassure me very much.

My guide had arranged for five "mean-looking" Huli Wig Men to trek with us for protection. All were decked out in their famous "wigs" and war-painted faces. In their hands were bows and arrows, which left me with the distinct impression that real danger lay ahead—not just a mock battle included in my tour price.

The warriors are called "Huli Wig Men" because during their battles they wear huge headpieces made of human hair. Their battles are festive events for the locals. In fact, clan warfare is often referred to as "Highland Football." Apparently it's all quite sporting, but men do get killed. The Huli culture is a "pay back" society. One clan's wronging of another calls for clan warfare. They fight over land, pigs and women. (The same things that rile many Western men, too.)

When the Hulis fight, each of the men dons his fanciest wig (see my picture on pages 58-59) and splashes his face in war paint before he goes off to do battle. But before fighting commences, each side must perform what they call a Sing-Sing, the ceremonial dance of the Bird-of-Paradise. Each team struts about in all its finery as they scream their war chants, trying to impress the opponent. Eventually battle begins. For weapons they use bows and arrows and sometimes machetes. The arrows are beautifully carved, and each warrior carries about a dozen. When I asked how they could do battle for any length of time with so few arrows, I was told that the agile young boys dashed to the front lines to retrieve spent arrows so they would have more ammunition to shoot back at the opposing "team." If the kids weren't fast enough, sometimes they died, too.

After a day's trekking we hadn't encountered any clan warfare.

We arrived at the village that would host our overnight stay. It was a walled compound surrounded by an enclosure of sticks and bamboo. The towering thatched-roof hut in the center was reserved for the village chief. On either side were smaller huts for each of his five wives and their children. The warriors and their families occupied the surrounding huts. Squealing pigs resided in the middle. And off to one side was the hut of the village witch doctor, where I was to spend the night as his guest.

Several village elders escorted me to his hut for formal introductions.

The witch doctor was a man of noteworthy presence. His skin was as black as pitch at midnight. His face was painted in red and white stripes radiating from his nose. He had wild bushy eyebrows and a massive head of black hair spiked in all directions. His nose was penetrated with a huge bone that looked as though it at one time might have belonged to the leg of a rhinoceros. Two-inch-round diameter stones were inserted in his drooping earlobes. Around his neck was a tight loop of cowrie shells and below that hung a chain of boar's teeth interspersed with dangling black feathers. His bare chest was painted with more red and white stripes, these emanating from his navel. Around his waist was a belt made of twisted hemp cord from which hung a massive clump of reeds to cover his private areas. Down the center of his back on each side of his spine ran a row of several hundred inch-long, horizontal scars that continued over his naked buttocks. His legs were hairy down to the knees, which were encircled by a band of grass reeds that hung just above his cowrie-shell ankle bracelets. His feet were bare. His long, agile fingers were laced with golden rings and in his left hand he carried a bloodstained machete. In the right hand he held a peace pipe.

With a rather schizophrenic look on his face, the witch doctor smiled at me.

He then invited me to stay for dinner—roasted pig I hoped, and not some form of cannibalism with me as desert.

Later, several village elders joined us. One of them

fired up an unusual looking pipe and passed it around. I didn't know what was being smoked, but before long everyone became glassy-eyed. I took a couple of hits, but of course I never inhaled, though I soon found myself sitting there in seventh heaven.

After a couple of hours of euphoria, I was escorted to my sleeping quarters, whereupon I started searching for rat droppings. Visions of that Irian Jaya rat festival were vivid in my mind. Dazed by the excitement of the evening—and perhaps the effects of that pipe—I had forgotten to ask the witch doctor if he knew some spell to cast over rats. Instead he had given me a cluster of ripe bananas in case hunger struck during the night.

Fearlessly, I prepared my bed and climbed under my trusty silk sleeping sheet, leaving the bananas on the small table next to my head. My flashlight was handy, but I'd forgotten to bring along a hammer for rat protection. Fortunately, by the time the alarm went off the next morning I hadn't seen or heard any of the pesky creatures. I did notice, however, that several bananas had been chewed half through while I slept. During the night those bananas had been sitting only a few inches from my face.

After several days of trekking, I arrived at my big splurge of the trip—the Ambua Lodge, a 300-dollar per night African safari type accommodation. Unless one wanted to keep staying with the witch doctor, there was no alternative in the area other than that lodge. Perhaps the price wasn't so bad when one considered that the hotel had to fly in its supplies by helicopter since truck convoys were usually ambushed and robbed. A couple of months earlier the last hotel manager had his hand chopped off by Huli warriors when he hesitated too long while opening the safe when the lodge was being robbed.

The new manager assured me, however, that there was nothing to worry about since the hotel had hired fifty Huli warriors as security guards. I could only hope that now they were on the inside they wouldn't turn renegade.

Later that evening, there was a little mishap at the lodge. A spark from the huge fireplace in the main dinning hall ignited the thatched roof, sending flames high into the night sky.

Those fifty Huli warriors must have thought the lodge was under attack—they came running and screaming with machetes and bows raised high. Assuming the stance of the Bird-of-Paradise, they commenced their Sing-Sing chanting and dancing, and in short order they were ready to duel. Eventually they realized the lodge wasn't being attacked after all.

Upon returning to my cabin, I discovered it had been robbed.

Never again would I leave ten thousand dollars of camera equipment in my room unattended. Why had I been so stupid? Papua New Guinea was a primitive country. Sophisticated cameras were way beyond what the average citizen might ever need or be able to comprehend. It's almost impossible to buy film in PNG.

But my cameras were safe at the foot of the bed.

My razor and a UCLA sweatshirt had been stolen.

8 RUSSIA

Leaping from poverty to world travel was thrilling. My pictures were selling wildly. I soon found myself criss-crossing the globe and visiting countries I'd only dreamed about.

Fast-forwarding forward . . .

Life in Russia today reflects the incongruity and bewilderment of a country migrating from meltdown to regeneration. No Russian city symbolizes this better than Moscow.

I'm glad I arrived in the city with a good pair of running shoes. Sounds crazy, but Moscow probably has the deepest subways and consequently the fastest subway escalators in the world—so speedy, in fact, that you have to start running before leaping onto these high-speed transports to hell. Well . . . maybe they don't descend all the way to purgatory. But you'll think so. Once safely on board these lickety-split escalators you'll invariably look down—into infinity. Imagine the longest escalator you've ever ridden and then multiply its length by at least ten and you'll have an impression of how deep Moscow's subways plunge into the earth's bowels. I was told that the city has a shallow water table and that's why the metro trains were buried so far beneath the plane upon which most of us terrestrial beings prefer to dwell. But remember, the subways were built when bomb shelters were on everyone's minds.

Khrushchev was no dummy.

About fifty feet before the end of a Moscow escalator's plunge you must gain momentum by running down the treads, preparing for a giant leap at the end. No, you don't really need to do this . . . unless you are willing to make an impromptu greeting with the concrete landing when it comes to an abrupt halt against your face.

And another thing . . .

When riding the subway trains, there's no easy way to figure out which station you've arrived at until the two sets of subway doors open—one set on the train, the other on the platform. Neither pair of doors has windows. When they open, there's about five seconds during the mad stampede of exiting passengers to decipher the Cyrillic alphabet on the opposite wall, which spells out the name of the station in what appears to be reverse, upside-down characters, before the doors snap shut on your nose. The best way to navigate Moscow's underworld is to count off the number of stops on the transit map between where you board the train and where you want to dismount.

Moscow's soul seems to be based on a deep-seated synergy of opposites. The whimsical, onion-domed architecture of St. Basil's Cathedral is juxtaposed with the impenetrable, bland walls of the Kremlin just a few dozen meters away. Exquisite Byzantine cathedrals coexist next to hideously drab residential blocks. The summers are plagued with stifling heat waves; the winters are besieged by subzero temperatures. Old-age pensioners remember food shortages and the disillusionment of recent decades while the new Mafioso-riche luxuriate in the untamed capitalistic indulgence in the city today.

Not so long ago Russia's militaristic might threatened doomsday scenarios. But centuries of oppression, despotism and the debauchery of Czarist Russia have given way to a brisk, unbridled economic advance on the future.

Despite my thrill at finally visiting Russia, I must admit that my nonstop traveling had frequently taken a toll on my body. Though my mind had pretty much become immune to culture shock, on occasion my bodily functions seemed to lag behind. There comes a time when every traveler direly wishes he or she had a huge dose of system-clogging Imodium—probably the world's best known diarrhea remedy.

By the time I arrived in Moscow I figured my stomach was made of cast iron. Surely by now I'd already sampled every culinary amoebae known to exist—everything from Montezuma's Revenge to Vietnam Vengeance to Delhi Belly. But it so happened that I was destined for the Cyrillic version of this rather urgent affliction, which I've since termed "Rushin' Revolution." As far as I know, it's atypical to have such inopportune abdominal misfortune in Russia—at least I've never heard of other travelers coming down with the symptoms I experienced on that fateful day. Let's just say I suddenly found myself in a very *big* hurry to find a men's room.

If only I'd consumed a couple more shots of Stolichnaya at lunch, maybe my stomach would have been impervious to the forthcoming invasion.

When the urge hit, I found myself walking past one of those drab, megalithic 1950s hotels, one that was built to impress the world with Russia's might—the kind of hotel that had five thousand rooms and a lobby the length of a couple of football fields with chandeliers the size of galactic explosions.

Surely there was a men's room somewhere!

I might interject at this point that I'd been somewhat apprehensive—if not downright scared—to visit Russia in the early '90s so soon after the Berlin Wall fell. There was a Wild West, winner-grabs-all flurry in the air, intensified by an already heightened sense of anxiety amidst ill reports about Russian Mafia who were gaining a measure of notoriety now that capitalism had begun to settle in. Forged documents, counterfeit money and stolen passports seemed to be the least of the offenses of the day. Numerous promulgating politicians, several overstuffed bankers and a few unwary tourists had either found their possessions stolen or worse yet, their bodies splattered against a wall. But Moscow is immense, somehow capable of absorbing such barbarity without hindering the daily life of the citizenry or the newfound tourism.

By the time I'd passed through the revolving front doors of that hotel my inner workings were *really* spinning under pressure to find some relief. Finally! There was a sign pointing to the WCs. I barreled down the stairs and burst through the doors and couldn't help noticing that this men's room was really enormous— there were at least two-hundred toilet stalls, or maybe by then my sanity had already been driven to extreme levels of delirium.

I charged toward the first stall, but—alas—the door latch was broken and couldn't be locked so I quickly moved to the next compartment. But that door latch was broken too. In fact, all the latches on the next six stall doors were either missing or broken. Perhaps they'd succumbed to aging malfunction or the lack of a fiscal budget to keep them repaired.

Not being able to wait another second, I charged into the next stall, dropped my pants before the door closed, stashed my camera bag on the shelf at the rear of the compartment and collapsed on the toilet seat in one fluid movement.

At last!

Though I was seriously engaged at that particular moment, I did notice the sound of someone entering. This was a big hotel. I didn't think much about the fact that some other gentleman would find this cavernous dungeon of a men's room. My body was in the unimpeded process of fluctuating from the depths of extreme pain to the heights of ethereal bliss—I was otherwise occupied. Little did I know that the guy who'd just come in was probably the one who had removed all the latches.

Suddenly—with a shocking explosion of sound—my stall door burst open. The man was diving at my pants, which were dropped to the floor. As you can imagine, this was enough to really scare the shit out of me.

But I came up fighting anyway.

The man was trying to extract my wallet from my pants pocket! Overwhelmed with fright, I lurched to my feet and started pounding him on the head even though I knew one should never try fighting off a mugger. Still, I was not about to lose my possessions—my dignity I'd already lost by standing up with my pants around my ankles.

I was screaming at the top of my lungs. It must have been a sight worth seeing—me slugging this guy while I was positioned in such a state of overexposure. I tried kicking him, but with my jeans gathered at my feet there wasn't much I could do. Though the would-be-robber was suffering furious blows from my fists, he did eventually yank the wallet from my pocket. He kept yelling in a gruff Russian accent, "Passport! Passport!"

I kept pounding his head.

Surely this mugger never had a victim resist with such vengeance. He didn't know that my passport was in my money belt, which I always wear in the back under my shirt out of sight—though everything else in front was fully open to view.

Maybe it was my fury that scared him off! Or maybe it was the odor that eventually made him drop my wallet and make a mad dash from the room.

I fell back on the toilet seat. But my work was already completed there. So I hurriedly yanked up my pants, gathered my camera bag and ran for my life.

Who needs Imodium anyway?

9 RED TAPE HASSLES

As far as X rays go, I never put film in my check-in luggage. Since 9/11 many countries are using X ray machines for checked luggage, machines that will literally fry film. In the United States it's usually possible to get hand inspection for carry-on film if you ask politely, especially if you have high-speed emulsions. I've discovered that many places in the world aren't so gracious when it comes to hand inspection, especially in Europe or any country where there's a war nearby.

Security in Israel is intense, as can be expected. At the airport I was interrogated for thirty minutes, and that was before my bags had even gone through the X-ray machine. I was traveling with a couple of friends. We were separated and each of us was asked myriad questions: "Where did you have dinner last night? In which hotel did you stay three days ago?" And so on. Then the security personnel huddled together and compared our answers. Fortunately for us, our responses must have jived. Who's complaining? Such delays are preferable to being blown out of the sky by terrorist bombs.

Though it might not help much, I use lead bags (available at most pro camera stores) for my film— three bags stuffed inside each other because of my paranoia. Many have said that X-ray machines for hand-carry baggage won't hurt most film unless it's high-speed. Still, it gives me great satisfaction to not believe this, even though it's most likely true. Nevertheless, I'm leery of antiquated machines in Third World countries, machines that might not have been inspected or calibrated for decades. So I continue to use my "custom-made" triple-layer X-ray bag. At least I feel good about the whole debilitating X-ray process.

It's best to register camera equipment at the customs counter before leaving your home country. Obviously you wouldn't want to pay duty on photo gear when coming back home. When leaving the States, I always visit the Customs counter the day before flying because, invariably, the one-and-only Customs person on duty will be on a coffee break during the last ten minutes before my flight is scheduled to depart, which has happened to me more than once. As required, I take all my equipment with me to prove my serial numbers, though in my experience Customs officials rarely ask to see every piece of the gear—a few random items at most. It seems that if they think someone is really a professional photographer (depends on how you talk the talk), then they might trust that all the equipment on your list is in your possession. It would be wise to bring everything just in case, along with a list of each item by serial number. It's much faster that way when filling out the declaration form. Though seemingly casual, customs inspectors are highly trained to spot frauds.

Another problem is that travel documents can be stolen. As a backup to my originals, I always carry photocopies of my passport ID pages and the visas that are attached or stamped inside. That way, if I were to be mugged, it would be easier to have a new passport issued at the local American embassy and to at least try to prove I'd already been officially authorized to be in the country in which I'd lost it. Ditto for my airline tickets and any other important documents, even traveler's checks. This includes my little yellow "International Certificate of Vaccination As Approved By The World Health Organization" in which is listed every vaccination I've had since I was born—almost—including my immunity to Japanese Encephalitis and my eyeglass prescription. I keep extra copies of these documents in my money belt, my camera bag and my backpack and in some cases my underwear.

Obviously I'm very paranoid—and anal retentive.

By the way, it's possible to have two legal USA passports, assuming you are a U.S. citizen, though it takes some effort to obtain the second one. I once visited ten countries in a row—passport required, of course—while my second passport was in London for eight weeks in the hands of an expert visa service. In my absence, and on my behalf, they acquired five rather difficult to obtain visas to Russia, China, Uzbekistan, Tajikistan and Pakistan—a Silk Road trip I had planned. I was amazed that the visa service bureau was able to process those visas for me in such short order—meanwhile my other travels continued unimpeded. If you do have two passports, however, *never* let the immigration officials see both of them at the same time or you'll have a lot of explaining to do. More important, make sure you exit a country with the same passport you entered with . . . or you might find yourself in deep trouble if the immigration stamps don't match.

Nowadays I usually don't plan trips in too much

detail prior to my departure. And I almost never read guidebooks thoroughly before I leave. I buy them, yes. But usually there's never enough time to look at them until after boarding the plane. Making precise advance hotel reservations is difficult because I never know how long I might want to stay in each city. If the weather is bad or my favorite travel icon is covered with scaffolding, I might want to move on.

Who needs reservations anyway?

It's guaranteed that *all* the hotels in just about any guidebook to major cities are fully booked months in advance. Why? Simply because those hotels are listed in the guidebooks. Can you imagine how many accommodations exist in a city like Paris? Guess how many are listed in the guidebooks? Maybe only fifty at most. Tens of thousands of tourists arrive in Paris everyday . . . and they each have one of those trusty guidebooks in hand. Every hotel they call is fully booked. There are hundreds of half-empty hotels on any given day in Paris that aren't even listed in the guidebooks. Just flip through the yellow pages to find them. *Page Juene, en francias.*

To make life easier at X-ray machines around the world, I always make sure my film is visible. A hundred 35mm rolls will fit into a one-gallon clear plastic zippered bag which I double, reversing one bag into the other before putting this assembly inside the lead bag. When the security person asks me to open my triple-layer-X-ray-proof-lead-bag-because-his-X-ray-machine-can't-see-through-the-damn-thing, the trusty zipper of the plastic bag inside, since it's doubled, won't come loose, thus scattering a hundred rolls of film under the X-ray machine, which has also happened to me two or three times.

You probably shouldn't worry too much about all this. During more than five hundred international flights over the past decade, I've only had one exasperatingly bad experience with X-ray problems. That was at the airport in Vilnius, Lithuania. An over-exuberant security guard didn't seem to believe that each of the three hundred film canisters I presented wasn't stuffed with a plastic explosive. Randomly selecting one roll of film from the pile, I removed the little one-inch piece of Scotch # 202 masking tape from the film leader, then pulled the entire roll of unexposed film from the cassette for his inspection. The security man finally acknowledged my innocence and let me pass.

I had thought that flying out of Lithuania would be a snap compared to what I went through getting into the country. A week earlier I hadn't known my night train from Warsaw would be passing through a corner of the former Russian enclave, now independent Belarus. As I lay comfortably in my berth, the train's clickety-clack had finally lulled me into a very deep sleep.

In the middle of the night the train screeched to a halt, almost tossing me to the floor. Loud Russian voices could be heard in the corridor; my couchette door was thrust open.

Belarus passport control.

The country was still a communist regime, and by the brusque manner of these burly border guards, they must have believed the KGB was alive and well. Didn't they know the Berlin Wall fell years ago?

Had the train not been stopped, we could have traversed this leg of the journey in less than an hour. In the end it took three hours and six passport checkpoints to cross that tiny corner of Belarus before my arrival to Lithuania. Declaration forms were rudely shoved in my face. I couldn't read the Cyrillic alphabet. No one but me spoke English. Finally I surmised they wanted me to list all my cash and personal belongings on their form. It was only the beginning of my second around-the-world trip. There were several thousand dollars in traveler's checks and cash in my money belt and now twenty thousand dollars of camera equipment in my bag, not to mention three hundred rolls of film in my pouch—quantities I wasn't too keen to list for obvious reasons.

I didn't know that a Belarus transit visa would be required, nor did I know that the night train was routed to pass through this narrow section of the country. My passport was confiscated in a flash. The inspector's intimidating stature, plus the gun bulging from his holster, left no doubt in my mind who was in charge. He insisted I leave my belongings on the train and come with him into the station's immigration office to fill out the proper paperwork, and he made it quite apparent there was no other choice but to come along.

The harsh, yellow light of a lone sodium-vapor street lamp cast my reluctant shadow on the train platform as I grudgingly followed the adamant border guard inside. I was led several flights up a dark stairway and directed to wait in a tiny room. A huge desk stood in the middle with piles of paperwork stacked haphazardly on top. No clerk was in sight. Five minutes, ten minutes passed. Where was the damned clerk? The train might depart at any minute. In the corner of the room was a closed door that appeared to be a closet, but from behind its confines I heard what sounded like a grunt and then a flush. Must be a toilet, I surmised. Surely the immigration officer would be with me shortly. By now fifteen minutes had passed. I brushed the perspiration from my forehead. The second hand of the clock on the wall labored by.

There were no windows in the room, no fresh air either. A train whistle blew. Another grunt and a flush. Railway cars clanged into each other. Imagining the worst, I could envision my train pulling from the station without me, my cameras disappearing into the night. "Hello," I yelled. Wasn't that damned immigration officer finished yet?

Finally a portly woman opened the little closet door and arrogantly marched into the room. Military stripes were on her sleeve; a badge was at her chest; a gun was at her waist. Her skirt strained at the seams.

A pungent odor wafted into the room.

I almost fainted trying to hold my breath. Though my vision was rapidly blurring, it was hard not to notice that the buttons on her uniform were straining under the pressure of her enormous girth. Her heavy shoes plodding across the concrete floor echoed in military cadence and her thick ankles bulged under the weight of each step. It was easy to imagine furniture being knocked askew by her rotund backside as she plowed through the room. Under her arm was a thick stack of reports, which she plopped on the cluttered desk. She had been sitting on the loo where she'd probably been committing to memory all the facts and figures in those volumes. Madam Starched Shirt looked at me with an unwelcoming scowl as she snarled in a heavy Russian accent, "I vould like to zee your passport." She brusquely yanked it from my hand.

I wanted my transit visa; I wanted to get out of there as fast as possible. I'd been jostled from a comfortable sleep and forced into this irritating situation during the middle of the night. It was challenging to remain calm, knowing that at any second my cameras might be stolen from the train. Nevertheless, there was indeed a funny side to this scenario, and now that I was fully awake, it was becoming easier see.

After the immigration officer snatched the passport from my hand, she began slowly inspecting each page. A few seconds of aggravating silence dragged past. My sense of humor was being tested. *Speed this up, Lady*, I wanted to say. Maybe she sensed my impatience because she began flipping the pages even more slowly. She snorted, causing the enormous, hairy wart on the side of her nose to twitch.

My vivid imagination started spinning wild visions about her and the unsavory pastimes she most likely pursued. Her previous employment couldn't possibly have been for The Goodwill Friendship Exchange Committee. She'd probably come to her present job straight from the local gulag, where she most likely took delight in extricating answers from uncooperative tourists with elaborate pain-induced methods.

In a gruff voice, she issued her next expletive, "Vy iss dere so many stamps in ziss passport?" She tilted her head back—an accusing scowl on her face, one eyebrow lifted higher than the other, her forehead strained into wrinkles of distrust.

Unable to restrain myself, I responded, "I have so

many stamps in my passport because I've been to so many countries."

She leaned toward me. Her beady eyes sent cold shivers up my spine, giving me the distinct impression she wasn't pleased with my curt response.

"I zee you hafe been een Russia vonce already." Her emphatic tone scared me. "And wat iss zee nature of ziss veeseet to Belarus?" She snorted with an authoritative air that was indicative of her enormous presence.

Perhaps it was best for me to adopt a more cooperative tone. "I'm not planning to visit Belarus. In fact, I had no idea the train passed through your country." She must have interpreted my comment as being rather snide. The interrogation continued relentlessly with numerous nonessential questions followed by my countless irrelevant answers. I glanced at the clock. Thirty minutes since I'd left the train. Her thoroughness seemed to indicate she could keep me there forever. I had to empty every pocket.

Another train clamored from the station.

My mind spun with crazy imaginings. Lord knows what method of inducing pain or techniques of subjugation this woman might enjoy. She reached to pull something from her desk drawer. What instruments of punishment might she have inside?

She commanded, "You vill geeve me forty-five dollars, pleeeze, for zee tranzit visah!"

I gladly shelled out the money before she changed her mind. STAMP. I grabbed my passport and raced toward the door. But something motivated me to take measure of my haste. Turning to look over my shoulder, I saw that the woman's face was filled with a knowing smile.

I was confused.

Had I misjudged her? Had she known all along that the train wouldn't leave without me? Maybe my imagination—and my anxiety—had painted the wrong picture.

Still, driven by fear, I bounded out the door and shot down four flights of stairs. But nothing looked familiar. A maze of dark hallways lay before me. This must be the basement. Maybe I had descended too far.

Precious seconds ticked away; the train might already have left.

Turning back, I bolted up the stairs three steps at a time to the next level. I burst through the exit and onto the platform. Racing forward, I leaped into the train, then charged down the corridor and into my sleeping compartment only to discover that all my camera equipment was . . . still there. Collapsing into my bunk, I tried to catch my breath, letting out a deep sigh of relief.

The train rested—tranquilly, sleepily—a good thirty seconds before the whistle blew, wheels creaked, cars lurched, and the slumberous locomotive began to heave itself forward, clanking and shuddering as it dragged away from the station.

To the wire again.

I relaxed into my couchette and into the motion of the swaying train, trying to leave memories of the past hour behind. But my mind wouldn't let me off that easily.

Perhaps my judgment had been too hasty.

The woman's final warm smile haunted me long into the night.

NEXT PAGE: STATUE OF LIBERTY AND
THE WORLD TRADE CENTER TOWERS, NEW YORK

GLEN ALLISON

GONDOLAS AT SUNSET, VENICE, ITAL

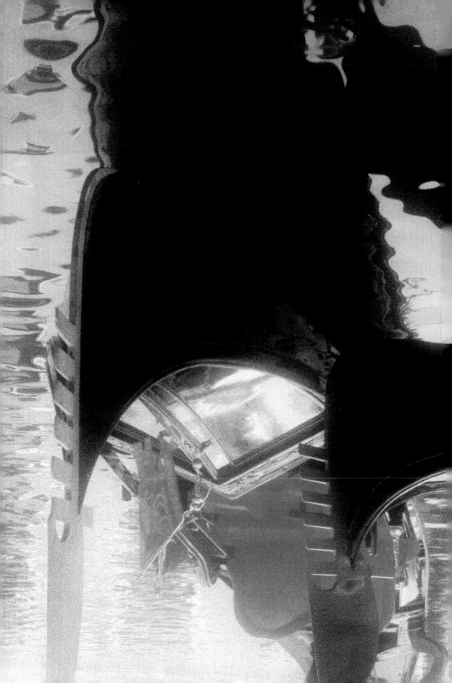

GOLDEN STATUE
WAT PHRA KAEW
GRAND PALACE
BANGKOK

RICE TERRACES, BA

WOMEN WITH CEREMONIAL OFFERINGS, BA

BA
BARON
DRAGO
DANC

EMATION CEREMONY, BALI

NEON SIGNS SHANGHAI CHINA

POTALA PALACE, LHASA, TIBET

MA
DOGON MUD CLIFF VILLAGE, BANDIAGAR

MASKED DOGON FUNERAL DANCERS, MA.

10 THAILAND

Snarled traffic, dismal pollution and the sweat-drenching heat of Bangkok can overpower just about any traveler. Nevertheless, Thailand's frenetic rush into the trappings of the Western world seems not to have tarnished the gentle-hearted nature of its inhabitants, their appreciation for life or their genuine respect for others. Thai culture is all the more complex for its rich Buddhist history, glittering temples and risqué massage parlors—reverent faith juxtaposed with the seamy, irreverent sex trade for which the country has become famous. The gilded Buddhas and orange-robed monks, the spicy cuisine and elegant Thai dance—all paint an exotic portrait of this beguiling country for those who are willing to embrace the seductive pull of its culture and its chaos.

Open-sided three-wheel vehicles, called tuk-tuks, roar through the streets, leaving passengers clinging to their seats amid the deafening noise of the vehicles' two-stroke engines. Millions of these "taxis" whiz by left and right, zipping between cars, dodging pedestrians or making sporadic U-turns midstream. In hopes of staying alive to endure such street thrills even one more day, many drivers and most of the traffic cops wear facemasks to block out the ever-present exhaust fumes. Nervy as they are, even tuk-tuk drivers get stuck in

Bangkok's traffic-clogged maze of streets and alleyways, so the fastest way to traverse the city is by motorcycle taxi—if you are brave enough to risk the challenge. Just keep your knees tucked in tight. Wearing protective football padding might not be a bad idea either.

My first visit to this engaging nation found me surrounded by machine guns on the rooftop of an army complex at the height of the military coup of February 1991. A bottle of Sang Son whiskey and a thousand-baht note for each of the two soldiers guarding me had bought my way up to Bangkok's best vantage point to photograph the Grand Palace at twilight.

That day the roadways were crawling with military vehicles and tense armed guards who seemed to be suspicious of every moving body on the street, including mine. The rifle-shaped tripod bag slung over my shoulder must have made me appear like a rather suspicious character. I was aggressively searched for weapons more than once.

In a move that shut down the local press for a day and curtailed public assembly, the Thai military shocked observers around the globe by toppling the democratically elected civilian government in a bloodless coup, though that fact didn't make it any less frightening for me. This was one of Thailand's ten successful coups out of nineteen attempts since the 1930s and I sure didn't want to be trapped in the middle of it. But there had to be a way to shoot my much sought after photo despite the risks and dangers of the night. That's where the whiskey and baht bribes came into play.

One must be bold.

The Grand Palace and its adjoining temple complex,

GLEN ALLISON

Wat Phra Kaew, is Bangkok's most iconic landmark. Endless golden chedis, ornately carved spires and mirror-laced towering facades shimmer with extensive night lighting. (See my photo, pages 60-61.) To capture the essence of this grandeur on film is every travel photographer's challenge—a formidable task, I was discovering, since I was convinced a high perch would prove the best vantage point. Current events made me afraid that a chartered helicopter would probably be shot out of the sky by missiles launched from the military buildings across the street. The fidgety mood of heavily armed troops patrolling nearby gave me pause.

Getting up to that rooftop with my cameras proved rather easy, however, especially considering that my forty-dollar bribe in Thai baht probably represented a month's salary for each of the two soldiers who had their guns pointed at me. But getting down from that rooftop proved to be a bit more hair-raising.

At numerous restaurants in the city, I had already surmised that the typical Thai male loves to consume large quantities of Sang Son whiskey, and these two chaps beside me soon validated that observation. I must admit that they seemed rather anxious, if not outright scared, to be sneaking me into that military compound at the height of a coup. But no doubt the very large bottle of Sang Son in my bag and the flash of large bills in my hand coaxed them to take the risk.

Hopefully I'd get out of this alive.

The adventure began soon after my two bodyguards distracted several other soldiers who stood sentry at the gate. My new compatriots—or should I say machine-gun-toting conspirators—hurried me around the barricades when no one was looking and down the side of the military building where we dashed into a stairway that led to the roof.

Adrenaline-pumped fanaticism and four flights of stairs left me gasping for breath once we made it to the top. Surely this was international espionage at its height.

Long ago I learned to engage nervous guards in the excitement of my photo endeavors. The first step was to let them look through the viewfinder. The second step was to get them drunk.

After I hurriedly rigged my tripod with camera and lens, one soldier propped his machine gun against the leg of my tripod and stretched to take a peek through the lens. His face lit up almost as brightly as the nearby Grand Palace, which was aglow in dazzling reflections and spotlights. The other soldier followed suit, laying his machine gun aside when he, too, lifted his eye to the viewfinder.

Meanwhile, I unscrewed the cap from the bottle of whiskey and passed it to my newfound friends, and we commenced taking turns downing Sang Son shooters straight from the bottle for the next thirty minutes as the deepening twilight sky enveloped the temple spires across the street.

My pictures would be fantastic.

When the photos were finished, the bottle of whiskey was almost empty. It was time to get off that roof. That's when the real fun began. I had over indulged and was feeling all the braver for it.

My barroom buddies grabbed their weapons.

One of the soldiers lifted a finger to his lips to shush

our boisterous laughter and we headed to the stairwell. Bear in mind that the entire evening had transpired via sign language. But, hey! Money talks.

Tiptoeing in the darkness, we made our way down. But when we stepped outside, to our surprise a convoy of military vehicles was pulling into the parking lot. Amidst a flurry of excitement soldiers scurried about, their weapons drawn. Maybe a top-brass general had arrived to take charge. My pals got real nervous. They must have feared we'd be facing a firing squad if it were discovered they had sneaked me onto the premises. We ducked behind some bushes till all the commotion died down. Then we made a mad dash for the front gate. I could almost hear my heart throbbing against my chest. Naturally, we were caught red-handed before we could escape. Fortunately it took only another thousand-baht note to compel the soldier at the security kiosk to let us go free.

Outside the compound my two buddies and I dashed a block down the street. When safely out of view, we stopped to catch our breath. I pulled the almost empty bottle of Sang Son whisky from my bag to share the last hit in celebration of our escape. With broad smiles on our faces and hearty pats on the back, we waved goodbye. Then I grabbed the first tuk-tuk that zoomed past, leaving an exhaust trail of fumes behind me in the lingering night.

The Thais are inherently tolerant people, but a word of warning: never disparage their monarchy or their Buddhist religion. The royal family is held in tremendous esteem.

A litany of other do's and don'ts:

Buddha images are sacred. It would be highly frowned upon to pose for pictures in front of them, nor are they to be touched or clambered upon. Also, there might be a plethora of exotic-looking monks on the streets, but women should never touch them, nor should monks be handed anything directly by those of the opposite sex. Objects to be given them by the feminine gender should be placed within their reach or put into the monk's "receiving cloth."

Social etiquette requires that the feet not be pointed at anyone or used to point things out, nor should you prop your feet on chairs or tables when sitting. And never, never touch anyone with your feet or step over anyone. Take your shoes off when entering temples or when visiting people's homes. Don't sit on pillows meant for the head and don't touch people's heads with your hands. That means no ruffling of any kid's hair. Any slip-ups should be immediately apologized for or you'll be thought of as being extremely rude and crass.

Leaving the frenzied dynamism of Bangkok behind, I made my way to Chiang Mai—the moated, formerly walled capital of the north. This once quaint city had long since spilled over those walls with the onslaught of international backpackers a couple of decades ago who were seeking the serenity of the nearby hill tribe lifestyle—or perhaps the solace of illicit drugs.

It was incredibly hot on my first day in town. The sky was clear and it hadn't rained for months.

Strangely, my tuk-tuk driver was wearing a transparent plastic raincoat.

When I leaned forward to ask why, he mentioned something about the Songkran Water Festival, which was beginning that day. I had no idea what was in store for me. We whizzed past some kids with large buckets. Suddenly they flung the contents at us. I was drenched.

What the hell was that all about?

The driver laughed uproariously. Fortunately my cameras were still in the waterproof camera bag at my feet. Up ahead I saw several teenagers armed with giant squirt pistols. They took aim as we zoomed by. Were these people crazy? I was saturated once more.

"We do this each year," the driver yelled, "on the thirteenth of April." Glee filled his mischievous eyes. He whipped our tuk-tuk around a corner and headed straight toward a group of young girls with water hoses gushing in our direction. We were thoroughly soaked again.

This was starting to be fun.

The driver hit the brakes and wheeled our tuk-tuk through a hasty U-turn, then headed back toward the girls for another generous outpouring of their hospitality. I braced my foot against the side of the tuk-tuk for the approaching torrential downpour.

I always store gallon-sized, clear plastic zippered bags under my lenses for extra padding and emergencies. Yanking one out, I shoved a camera inside and zipped it up tight.

This water fight just had to be documented on film.

An open-bedded small truck pulled up alongside us. Several kids in the back, with large buckets in their hands, hovered over what appeared to be a five-hundred-gallon barrel. Within seconds I was doused by another tidal wave in the face—bucket after bucket. My driver made sure we cruised alongside that truck for at least three more very wet blocks.

With my finger pressed down on the motor-drive button, I raised my sealed-up camera and fired off several frames without even looking through the viewfinder.

The entire city had gone mad.

Taxis and tuk-tuks and motorbikes circled wildly through the streets and over the sidewalks, horns blaring, water blasting in everyone's faces. Car doors were being yanked open at traffic intersections and the passengers inside were getting doused with buckets of water. (See my photos on page 62, which give testament to the madness.)

My driver became a fanatic, driving straight toward every probable inundation he could find. An hour later at the end of our submarine ride, he was paid with sopping wet baht, which he didn't seem to mind.

The streets were awash with water and laughter and screams. When I finally made it back to my hotel that night, even the desk clerk was dripping.

Next time I'm in Chiang Mai on April thirteenth, I'll bring a Nikonos underwater camera along for the swim.

11 VIETNAM

The Vietnamese are extraordinarily resilient. They appear to have left behind the war-weary fatigue of the past, discarding bitter memories and replacing ill feelings toward the West with a headstrong economic leap toward the future. During the last decade the government relaxed its control and allowed a free market economy to develop. Despite the full-tilt entrepreneurial explosion in the cities, there still remains a huge gulf between rural and urban Vietnam in a nation where the per capital annual income is still less than a dollar per day.

The cities buzz with activity. Roadways are lined with shops and stalls, selling everything from dried fish and packaged noodles to sophisticated electronics, including wide-screen high-definition TVs. Products spill over onto the sidewalks, blocking the path of mobile vendors manning their stands-on-wheels as they vie with an endless procession of street-wise hawkers peddling their wares.

Despite the fever-pitched frenzy of commercialism that has seized the nation there's a downside to progress, as I learned on a recent visit. I'd read in the in-flight magazine that the number of motorbikes on the streets had increased by a whopping one third during the past year—this in a country that even six years ago, on my first visit, was already jammed with two-wheeled vehicular traffic. Most of the bikes had been old and beat up back then. But thanks to the expanding economy, all the bikes looked brand new today.

I discovered that the streets of Saigon were totally insane. The traffic was so jammed on Le Loi Street that it seemed impossible to get across the road without making a life-threatening mad dash. The intersections were utter chaos with motorbikes crisscrossing in a crazed procession of disorder without the benefit of traffic lights.

Following advice from my guidebook, I stepped off the curb and began walking slowly into the path of oncoming traffic!

In unison the drivers judged my leisurely pace and carefully slipped past me on either side as I nonchalantly strolled across the street. The trick is to never make an all-out dash through the onslaught of spiffy new motorbikes on any street in Vietnam.

If you do, you'll die.

Despite the hair-raising bustle of traffic, Vietnam is a beautiful, fun-loving destination, and in many respects still quite naive. Get there before every square inch of beachfront property is lined with high-rise hotels like those in Miami Beach. The process is already well under way. The country's economic development is in a powerful state of flux: conical hats and water-buffalo-drawn wooden plows are rapidly being overtaken by the fast pace of entrepreneurialism.

Hard-line communism has been replaced by flat-out capitalism with local inhabitants pouncing like vultures on new opportunities to make money. Unfortunately the ever-exploding tourist boom has made unwary travelers the recipients of a fair measure of this voracious pouncing.

Scam artists proliferate.

Numerous rip-offs over the years have honed my skills in spotting con artists and frauds. But when I arrived at the airport in Hanoi recently, a new one was pulled on me.

I thought I had learned all the lessons long ago. On my first trip to Southeast Asia, ten years earlier, a savvy taxicab driver in Hong Kong had bilked me out of a hundred dollars on a ten-dollar ride from the nearby Kai Tak airport into Kowloon—a lesson not soon to be forgotten. I later figured out that the man had adjusted the decimal point on his meter, moving it over one digit in his favor. Jet lag and first-time-visitor naiveté, along with the driver's wily ways, had conspired to deceive me. Leaving his car parked at the curb, he had come into the baggage claim area to solicit an unsuspecting customer, and naturally, I needed a taxi. He was a friendly chap and pointed out the long line of travelers waiting at the taxi queue as he explained that he never liked to wait in the driver's queue either. Lucky me, I'd arrive at my hotel all that much quicker. A fifteen-hour transpacific flight from L.A. to Hong Kong had left me fatigued, and a quick shower would feel great. The man was driving a real taxi with a light on top, a meter inside and a registration ID on the dashboard. Everything looked kosher to me. At the end of our journey into town it did seem a bit odd that the driver stopped across the street from my hotel instead of at the front door. But he'd kindly explained that he couldn't cross the center divider and if he went around the block it would only cost me more money. My pocket calculator wasn't handy and the neon-glitzed streets of Kowloon (photo on page 86) must have dazzled my travel-weary mind to the point of confusion. I hadn't realized I'd been hoodwinked until the taxi had already disappeared into the night.

More worldly wise now on my umpteenth visit to Southeast Asia and my fourth to Vietnam, I proceeded through the Hanoi airport terminal on the lookout for crafty types who were sure to approach me for transport into town. And sure enough, within fifteen seconds someone did. You must realize that Vietnam is not like, say, Los Angeles. Vietnamese crooks aren't out to take your money and then kill you just for the hell of it, so I wasn't overly concerned about my safety—just a fair price for my ride. Refusing to begin my visit to Hanoi with pessimism, I decided to give this guy the benefit of the doubt, at least for a few minutes.

Never let a taxi driver in a third-world country take your luggage as long as you can handle it by yourself. Once he's towing your bag, you're *his* customer and it will be all that much harder to disentangle yourself from him if the need arises. My backpack functions as a small canvas suitcase when the shoulder straps are zipped under the rear panel flap. And the recessed wheels and pop-out handle allow me to tow it along by myself when I'm on smooth terrain, and that's exactly what I did that day.

When we walked past the first lane of official taxis outside, and then a second row beyond that, my suspicions were confirmed. It was obvious we were heading to the parking lot and probably straight to this guy's beat-up family sedan.

Chickening out, I told the man I wanted a "real" taxi and turned to head back to the ones with the lights on top and the signs on the side. But the overzealous pseudo taxi driver grabbed my arm to restrain me and tried to drag me back. Boy, was this going to be a scene if he didn't let go. Yanking myself free, I fled across the traffic lane to the row of authentic taxis, all the while trying to fight off this belligerent driver's manhandling tactics and verbal abuse.

He blocked me from getting into the taxi and began yelling in Vietnamese at the other drivers who gathered around. I started looking for a cop. Eventually I managed to throw my luggage and myself into the back seat of the official taxi, slamming the door shut behind me. My new driver sped off, leaving the other man ranting and raving on the street.

Whew!

But we didn't get three blocks beyond the airport when the driver stomped on the brakes, bringing the car to an abrupt halt. Oh crap! What was happening now?

He looked over his shoulder and grinned at me. My body became tense, my breathing became ragged. He opened the door and proceeded to remove the magnetically held taxi light from the rooftop, then he climbed back inside and stashed it under the seat.

Even this wasn't a *real* taxi!

All I could do was laugh.

Admittedly not everyone you meet in Vietnam is out to rip you off, but the number of unscrupulous hustlers and con artists is on the rise since my first visit in 1995.

Beware.

After indulging in Hanoi's provincial ambience of charming French-era mansions, verdant parks and elegant boulevards for several days, an excursion to the emerald waters of Halong Bay seemed like the perfect antidote to the street merchants and hustlers jostling to position themselves between me and my money.

Speckled with more than three thousand fancifully shaped islands (and the occasional Chinese junk if you're lucky), Halong Bay is a serene respite providing a much-needed escape for city-weary travelers. This portion of the Bay of Tonkin has been designated as a United Nations World Heritage Site, and justly so, for its magical outcroppings of breathtaking limestone islets and hidden grottoes. Legend has it that the unusual land/seascape was fashioned by a mysterious nautical creature of monstrous proportions. "Ha Long" translates as "where the dragon descends into the sea."

Avoiding the street hawkers of Halong City, who were hell-bent on steering single men into sleazy massage parlor dives, I hopped on a boat straight to the isolated island of Cat Ba only to discover that its quaint fishing-boat-studded harbor was now surrounded by endless new hotels under construction and the same touts offering to guide me to the local pleasures of the night.

Instead I opted for a nice seafood dinner aboard one of several floating restaurants anchored a few hundred yards off shore. A conical-hatted old lady rowed me in her little dinghy across the harbor to my dining destination of choice with an arrangement to retrieve me in an hour. The amicable chef of the buoyant establishment promptly led me to an array of fishing nets submerged off the deck to one side, whereupon I chose my dinner from among the giant shrimp playing in the bay. The candlelight meal was delicious (the floating restaurant had no electricity) and the evening lingered. The beer was nice, too. When it came time to pay, it was obvious I was being gouged outrageously. Next time I'll negotiate before eating. Indignant, I refused to pay such a ridiculous price. Then I was informed that my boat lady would not be coming back for me unless I chose to acquiesce.

Swim or pay.

I paid.

My proclivity is to view life with a positive outlook and I tried to do so in this case. There are pros and cons to every situation, but clearly the times had changed during my six-year absence from Vietnam.

The cons had become pros.

12 BALI

Water dripped from the eave of my thatched-roof bungalow, which was perched on the edge of a series of cascading rice paddies. The evening's downpour must have tempted the frogs to come out in proliferation. I leaned against the rail of my second-floor balcony listening to the serenade of deep-throated frog choruses as I stared into the night. Water gurgled and splashed from one rice terrace level to the next just a few feet below.

Bali was magic.

My hotel, the Ibunda Inn on Monkey Forest Road in Ubud, would serve as a base for my explorations during the next few weeks. The natural beauty of the island was awesome. The Balinese believe that when they die and enter the afterworld, heaven will look exactly like Bali. Now I knew why. With that thought I moved inside my room and lay on the bed. Leaving the door open to the breeze and the sounds of the night, I slept.

I awoke to a brilliant sunrise and noticed that in my doorway lay a tiny bamboo basket filled with flower petals and a small portion of rice—a religious offering to the gods. Each morning such offerings adorn every doorway, every gate, every opening, everywhere in Bali—no exception. Such respect they have for their religion.

Spurred by the namesake of the road on which my

hotel was located, I couldn't resist visiting the monkey refuge in the forest less than a kilometer away. A street vendor sold me a large bunch of bananas at the entrance gate. About fifty feet inside the jungle I encountered my first confrontation.

A huge male monkey marched toward me, his eyes resolutely fixed on mine—and, of course, the bananas.

I glared back.

As though in some distorted Darwinian struggle of survival, neither of us allowed ourselves to budge during the stare down for the bananas. I was convinced that my determination exemplified the more developed aspect of our shared evolutionary strains, so I locked eyes with the primate in a visual dual of perseverance. I dared not blink first. Boldly, I moved a step closer in challenge.

The monkey's eyes went wild. And he screamed.

Then he charged me.

The entire bunch of bananas was relinquished post haste. The monkey had won the stand off. These little guys were definitely aggressive, and I decided to leave the world of animality in their domain.

I went back to my rented "jimmy" jeep and soon found my way out of the village, then headed north to probably the most exquisite, steeply-terraced rice paddies in the world. (See my photo on pages 64-65.) Even before I saw the old man working on the slopes below, I knew I had to stop for what would most likely be my best picture of the day. Though, as it turned out, that day would soon be filled with the most fabulous pictures I'd taken in my life.

The Balinese man raised his head. His wizened face

was dark brown and leathery, tanned dark by endless years working in the rice terraces, most likely. His sparkling eyes shone from underneath the rim of his conical straw hat. The old man motioned for me to follow him, and I couldn't resist. With great agility he led me across the terraces.

What a balancing act!

The slippery ledge under my feet was less that a foot wide. Slipping off on the uphill side would mean sinking into soggy mud up to my knees. But that would be better than falling to the next terrace a dozen feet below. Up ahead the old man gracefully leaped across a narrow stream with the agility of a trapeze artist.

Attempting the same feat, I fell in.

That's when I learned a very good lesson.

My money belt contained travel documents, airline tickets, passport, vaccination certificates and cash. Those items didn't fare too well when I slipped into the rushing stream and became submerged up to my waist. Fortunately my cameras and film survived the dunking. My photo gear was inside the waterproof camera bag on my back. Ever since that day I've always made sure my valuable paperwork is neatly tucked inside a gallon-size, clear plastic zippered bag, which I stuff inside my money belt. I bring extra plastic bags of all dimensions. They're handy for dozens of uses. If I'm traveling during monsoon season or in an outrigger canoe, or both, the clothes in my backpack are tightly enclosed in large plastic bags as well. Most backpacks aren't all that waterproof, especially if they're riding on top of a bus when the sky breaks loose and the driver won't stop for you to rescue your bag.

That day in Bali—after cleaning the mud from my legs—I spent an hour in the rice terraces with the little Balinese man, shooting a multitude of compositions with him climbing from level to level across the photogenic rice terraces with two rattan baskets filled with rice stalks balanced on either end of a bamboo pole straddling his shoulders. Afterwards he invited me to his village of thatch-roofed huts for their once-a-year harvest celebration to the rice gods. Descending the terraces to the bottom of the gorge, we crossed a rushing stream over a rickety bamboo bridge and then we followed a path that led to his village. Most likely there wouldn't be any other tourists this far off the main road.

The old guy told me his friends called him Wayan. Funny, I'd already met about fifty people with the same first name. My curiosity about his name being so common was soon clarified. He told me that in Bali all the children are given first names that reflect the sequence of their birth with that of the other kids in the family. All firstborns are named Wayan, whether male or female. The second born child is called Made (pronounced Mah-day), the third is Nyoman and the fourth is Ketut. Obviously a lot of people wind up with the same name.

It was about a half-hour trek to Wayan's village and along the way he explained that there are three levels of Balinese spoken language: high, middle and low. The status or social relationship between one speaker and another determines the level invoked. When speaking to a superior, high Balinese is used, though that person will reply to one of lesser stature in the low form. Middle Balinese is considered to be the most polite and is utilized to address strangers.

When we arrived at Wayan's village, the locals were already assembled for the festivities. Wayan introduced me to his friends, Wayan and Wayan and Wayan and Wayan, who were all four standing next to the temple entrance. Inside I met Wayan and Wayan who were both arranging some traditional musical instruments.

The village men wore pleated headbands tied in artful display, and they had patterned sarongs wrapped around their waists. Each carried Balinese musical instruments: a drum or a gong or a gamelan. The women wore brightly colored lace blouses and sarongs and had red or yellow sashes tied around the middle. Effortlessly, they balanced three-foot-high fruit-laden offerings on their heads. (See my photo, pages 66-67. This balancing act seems almost impossible.) Kids ran with streamers and flags. Several men carried fringed, bright yellow ceremonial umbrellas. Two boys, dressed in a Barong dragon costume (photo on page 68) draped between them, playfully chased along behind the procession to scare off the demons and evil spirits that might harm the rice crop, the old man explained.

I followed the excitement through the village and into the rice paddies where the procession made its way to the bottom of the terraces—Barong dragon and all. At the bottom, the villagers continued with much singing and dancing and the offering of ritualistic prayers in front of a small shrine to the rice gods. Concluding that part of the ceremony, everyone climbed back up the slippery terraces, me charging ahead to get the best photo angles while trying to keep my balance.

Back in the village, dark storm clouds swirled overhead, followed by an ominous—though timely—crack of thunder. Lightening streaked across the sky. Maybe the gods had decided to join the ceremony. A village elder held a chicken above a fresh coconut and, in one chop of his machete, severed the bird's head and the coconut together. Holding up the torso, he drained blood into the coconut juice, then he bowed and made his offering to the altar in praise of the gods. Another ear-piercing blast of thunder followed.

When the sky cleared and the rain ceased, the old man led me through the rice paddies to my car. The golden light of sunset sliced between the palm fronds to cut jagged shadows across the stepped terraces.

A tiny Hindu temple made of thatch and bamboo rose from the water in the middle of a rice paddy. I assumed it stood in honor of the rice gods watching over the newly planted terraces. Tiny rice stalks pierced the golden-colored water, seemingly in gesture of prayer to those gods.

The next day I continued my exploration of the island and was lucky enough to come across a tooth filing ceremony. The young man who endured the "celebration" lay prone in a makeshift dentist's chair, his mouth pried wide open—ready for the file. There didn't seem to be any anesthesia nearby. The Balinese consider the canine teeth to possess a nature that is animalistic. They believe that male humans must overcome their proclivity to bestiality, a life condition which manifests soon after one reaches puberty. (I doubt if any of us Westerners would disagree with their assessment.) So the young man's front teeth were being filed even.

I should mention that in Bali one can't rent a car

without an International Driver's License, which can easily be obtained in the States at just about any local auto club office for the price of ten dollars, plus two passport photos and a driver's license. Many countries don't require an International Driver's License, but for those that do, it's only valid when presented with the home country license in hand. An alternative in Bali is to use a valid Balinese driver's license. Obtaining one is relatively easy but it's a time-consuming hassle to get one, especially if you're on the other side of the island and must travel back to Denpasar to the main police station, like I had to do when I first arrived. It's a wise idea to keep a dozen extra passport photos in your money belt for just such unforeseen circumstances. Photographers may carry tons of photo gear, but we can easily find ourselves hard pressed to come up with an I.D. photo on short order.

A few days after getting the license I attended a cremation ceremony held in a remote village on the slopes of Bali's most revered mountain, Gunung Agung, long since a defunct volcano. It had rained heavily during the night. As I approached the village I heard the rumble of thunder and prepared myself for another deluge, but the sound was just that of ceremonial drums in the distance.

Family and friends of the deceased and a few dozen tourists marched up the trail to the cremation site. A procession of village women carried their offerings— towering displays precariously balanced on their heads. Several villagers pulled a wheeled wooden sarcophagus carved in the shape of a giant bull, the vehicle to transport the liberated soul back to heaven. The deceased's body lay wrapped up tightly inside like a mummy. Hoisted on the shoulders of about a hundred men was a huge tower made from bamboo. It was lavishly decorated in a dazzling array of golden paper and fringe and mirrors and silk and ornaments galore—a tower that symbolized the vastness of the cosmos and the eternal fusion of life with that of the universe, I was told. The structure's multitiered roofs represented the heavens.

Snapping several photos, I joined in with the crowd.

One would expect funeral ceremonies to be somber occasions conducted in an atmosphere of solemn dignity. On the contrary, today there was much excitement and joy as the men charged up the road with their tower, dangerously tipping and spinning it in an effort to disorient the deceased's soul so it wouldn't be able to find its way back home to disturb the living relatives. Much shouting and yelling and laughter added to the confusion.

I chased around the procession trying to capture all the merriment and excitement on film. Then I tripped in a hole and fell to the ground, smashing one of my cameras against a rock. For a brief moment the crowd stared at me. My lens shade had popped off. The lens now seemed a bit wobbly, but other than that I pulled myself together, then brushed off the dirt and the embarrassment and kept shooting.

At the cremation site bamboo gamelans were played while the replica of the bull was carefully lifted to the top of the funeral pyre. An effigy of the deceased was placed at the front of the platform. The sarcophagus was opened and the body was anointed with pots of holy water, and then the pots were smashed. A pair of white birds was released, which symbolized the release of the soul to the heavens. As explained to me by one of the villagers, letters of introduction to the gods were placed inside the sarcophagus along with an envelope filled with money in payment to Yama, the god of the underworld—just in case the deceased might have committed a few evil deeds while he was alive.

The Balinese are very superstitious.

The funeral pyre was set aflame. (See the photo on page 69.) The blaze quickly engulfed the canopy, flames soaring into the sky. No tears were shed. No grief was shown. To do so might disturb the soul so much that it might not want to leave this earthly realm.

Rushing through the crowd, I framed pictures of the fiery spectacle. It would only last a few minutes. Eventually the shroud-wrapped body dropped from the belly of the wooden bull down to the platform, its protective cloth covering singed away . . . arms and legs waving, almost sadly, at the wind and flames. I lowered my camera long before the last ashes lost their glow.

After the heat dissipated, family members gathered the ashes to be thrown into the sea. Ultimately the physical remains would be restored to the five elements of nature, which the Balinese call *pancamahabhuta*—earth, wind, fire, water and ether. The soul is thus freed. If evil karma existed, they believe the deceased must now pass through purgatory for punishment and torture in order for the soul to be cleansed. (Not too different from Western beliefs, except we have to stay in hell for all eternity if we've been bad.)

A final Balinese funeral ceremony is held years later. (I couldn't wait around that long.) Apparently the deceased's soul is called back from the sea, and then it is somehow transported to a revered mountain temple for more ritual formality before it's released into the heavens to become deified for all eternity.

The fiery Balinese cremation I witnessed that day will remain indelibly burned into my memory.

A couple of centuries ago, when noblemen or kings died, their wives and concubines were thrown into the fire too.

Fortunately . . . times have changed.

13 SULAWESI

The razor-sharp blade caught the sun's reflection. One violent slash and the neck muscles were ripped open, straight through the jugular vein. Blood gushed and the world began to spin. There was a moment of panic and struggle. And terrified eyes. But death came quickly. The Tana Toraja tribesmen pounced on the body and efficiently carved it into small pieces—an offering to their revered and highly worshipped ancestors.

A water buffalo had been sacrificed.

Two days earlier, I had boarded a Garuda jet, leaving Bali on a flight to Ujung Pandang, the capital of Sulawesi. Then I headed north into Toraja country. Indonesia is composed of thirteen thousand islands stretching over three thousand miles, from the Papua New Guinea border in the east and beyond Singapore to Sumatra in the west. The country has three hundred distinct ethnic groups speaking just as many languages. The Tana Toraja is one of the more unusual Indonesian tribal groups.

The tribe lives in bamboo dwellings called "tongkonan" with rooflines that resemble the hull of a boat. These ship like constructions have immense elongated roofs. Their profiles are studded across the countryside throughout the Tana Toraja region. Built of bamboo and wood, these stilted structures have façades covered in painted designs and carved shapes. A row of pig jaws might be used for exterior decoration. Several water buffalo skulls with horns usually complete the motif.

Of even more interest are the peculiar funeral ceremonies of the Tana Toraja and their mysterious ancestral burial caves that resemble a Halloween night spectacle. It's not unusual for families to postpone funerals for months or even years after their loved ones have departed . . . while the families save their money to conduct extravagant funeral ceremonies. In the interim they keep the bodies prominently displayed in the house. Elaborate bamboo constructions are built to accommodate hordes of arriving guests. Many stay for days and days since funeral celebrations can go on for weeks, depending on the wealth of the family. The Indonesian government has tried to discourage these festivities, which place such a tremendous financial burden on the families.

While slaughter of water buffalo might at first seem rather pagan, it's easy to imagine the Torajans would need tons of meat to feed the hundreds of people who attend their funerals with celebrations lasting for days on end. It's more efficient to have the meat simply walk up the mountains to the funeral sites. There aren't any refrigerators up there. The animals are slaughtered daily as needed. Sometimes as many as a hundred water buffalo might be sacrificed at these events. It's a macabre spectacle seeing dozens of slaughtered buffalo lying in crimson pools of blood. Once the animals are carved up, the heads are sent to the home of the deceased person's family. The livers go to the house where the dead person was born. Other body parts are distributed to guests attending the funeral according to their social rank.

Off to my left I heard several sharp pig squeals. They were being slaughtered too, and their carcasses quickly carved up and placed into a huge caldron—the beginnings of a tasty stew.

Continuing the slaughter ceremony, large wicker cages were uncovered to release feisty roosters for a rousing cockfight. Celebrants gathered round to cheer for their favorite feathered contender. Razorblades were strapped to the cocky birds' legs. In short order more splattering blood was added to the festivities.

Thus honored with such huge quantities of sacrificial blood, it was believed that the gods would accord their good will to the relatives of the deceased. Enhancing the spirit of celebration, the funeral attendees consumed barrel after barrel of potent *tuak* rice wine, the local version of home brew.

Tourists are quite welcome to attend Torajan funerals—if they have the stomach for it.

Standing next to one of the hastily constructed bamboo shelters at the funeral compound, I discreetly shot pictures. Off to one side a few kids were playing with dead buffalo heads. Colorfully dressed young girls in traditional garb served snacks, as well as large quantities of tuak to the guests. Women wearing huge conical rattan hats filed by. Then the bereaved family and friends and relatives, all dressed in black, bore gifts and food offerings as they made their procession past the elaborate, hand-carved wooden casket of the deceased. The embalmed body, I learned, had been kept on display in the family home for a couple of years while money was being saved for this grand celebration. During the waiting period, the dead person wasn't really considered as dead—not until after the funeral ceremony. The family brought food to the body at mealtimes and addressed it with dignity and respect as if the deceased were still alive.

Many celebrants at the ceremony that day had brought along a gift water buffalo. Attendees bearing live presents had to pass by a bamboo hut, where stood the taxman, who collected the government duty levied on such gifts.

On a side note, I read that when babies die, their bodies are placed upright in niches carved in the trunks of large trees. Nourished by tree sap, it's believed that the babies will continue to grow, soon returning to the *puya* heaven where they can prepare for rebirth on earth.

I visited several Torajan ancestral burial caves, which were built in natural water-cut grottoes under hanging cliffs. In rock-hewn niches next to the entrances stood dozens of hand-carved wooden effigies known locally as *tau tau*. (Photo on page 72.) Sculpted in the image of and dressed to resemble those who had already departed for the next world, they stood in a gallery as ghostly protectors in commune with the dead. With hands outstretched, the tau tau appeared to be waiting for offerings to satisfy the souls of the deceased.

Inside the caves were dozens of ancient, intricately carved hanging coffins. A few appeared to have cracked open with age. Eerily, several sculls had been placed in the gaping holes. Rows of dark hollow eyes glared down at me, as they did upon whomever might venture into these forbidden surroundings.

It was spooky.

It was a good time to get the hell out of there.

14 CHINA

In China today there's an uncanny openness to Western influence, which seems to function efficiently side-by-side with the inflexible posturing of hard-line Communism we've read so much about in newspapers or seen on CNN.

During my first visit to Shanghai, I was overwhelmed by the throbbing chaos of humanity on the streets (photo on pages 70-71) and the wall-to-wall building construction under way. Surely the city will soon rival Hong Kong in its grab for economic prowess. Shanghai's skyline is monopolized by a sea of looming construction cranes with building activity persisting twenty-four hours a day. It's not unusual to see bamboo-scaffolding-clad, high-rise skeletons blazing in floodlight with hard-hatted construction workers working through the night—the clamor of jackhammers reverberating in every corner of the city. Make sure you choose your hotel relative to nearby construction sites. However, avoiding the rigors of sleepless nights might be next to impossible with a reported one-fifth of the world's construction sites located in Shanghai these days.

The city fathers, seemingly uninfluenced by the limitation of civic restraint—or potential uprisings by displaced, disgruntled local inhabitants—appear to

GLEN ALLISON

have no qualms plowing down entire neighborhoods to make way for massive urban renewal projects. Your favorite corner shop might not be there in the morning. Or an elevated six-lane freeway might be brushing your third-floor apartment window next week.

Smart shopping districts have cropped up overnight. Louis Vuiton, Gucci and Yves St. Laurent boutiques are as common to the metropolitan streetscape as they are in New York, London, Paris or Milano. Stressed-out Chinese urbanites barely have time to grab fast-food lunches at McDonald's while talking endlessly on their cell phones. There's even a KFC at the foot of the Great Wall of China just outside Beijing.

It's still possible to experience oriental charm in the hidden pockets of China's major cities, but it's now almost impossible to escape the encroaching influence of the West. There's the occasional translation faux pas. While strolling through the Yu Gardens in Shanghai (after grabbing a tall Café Latte at the nearby Starbucks), I came upon a much-hoped-for sign pointing to the nearest WC, fortunately for my over-pressured bladder. Hurriedly following a winding path through the bushes, I soon found two WCs to choose from—Men's Closet and Women's Closet.

My most unusual encounter in China was with a South African gentleman from Cape Town.

Fearing a translation nightmare if I tried to navigate the country on my own, I had decided to sign up for a group tour on this, my first visit to China. My travel company of choice only offered double-room occupancy and my budget at the time would not allow me the luxury of paying twice to go by myself. Unless I was the odd man out, I'd probably be stuck with a roommate.

After I arrived at my hotel in Shanghai and proceeded to my room, it became obvious that the chap I'd be rooming with during my three-week tour had already checked in. His bed was strewn with plastic bags stuffed with strange items I would soon become familiar with.

It was almost noon, not too early to visit the restaurant downstairs for lunch and a beer. The maitre d' escorted me past a couple of bronze dragons to my table. Circling the perimeter of the room was an arc of booths, each with a red Chinese lantern casting a crimson shimmer of light on the patrons' faces. I spotted one Westerner among the diners and assumed he must be my roommate. The elderly gentleman had been served a noontime feast. When I approached his table, he was just swallowing a bite of Peking duck rolled in a crepe and dripping with plum sauce.

"Excuse me," I inquired, "are you in the Adventure Odyssey tour group? If so, maybe you're my roommate."

"Yes, I am," the man replied. "My name is Humphrey." He wiped a drip of plum sauce from his chin with a napkin. "Do you know there are 334 steps from this table back to our room?" he exclaimed.

"Really!" I was intrigued and could only wonder what might be in store for me for the duration of the trip.

Humphrey was a seventy-eight-year-old white South African, who had a penchant for counting. He graciously implored me to join in the feast that lay before him. "You must have a bite of this Peking duck," then he rolled a crepe around several strips of duck and spooned on some plum sauce. "It's great with Tsing Tao beer," he insisted. He reached for an extra glass. "You know, I've only been in China for a couple of hours," he said as he neatly tucked the crepe around the duck, "and so far I've counted twenty-seven different makes of Chinese automobiles."

I could tell this trip was going to be fascinating.

Humphrey insisted we order more food. Culinary experiences in China can be exotic; the Chinese eat things many people in the rest of the world might not try. I'd read in my guidebook that one could find caged dogs and cats in the street markets and that these cuddly creatures weren't being sold as pets. The author warned readers not to be disturbed by piles of dried rodents on display for those discerning Chinese culinary aficiona-dos perusing the outdoor markets for interesting dinner selections.

Trying to block those thoughts, I carefully scru-tinized the menu Humphrey handed me. Bird's Nest Soup, Fish Head Stew, Creamed Duck's Feet, Dog Meat Sausages with Garlic, Pig Brain Casserole, Fried Fish Balls, and Spicy Chicken Penises with Sticky Rice—liter-ally. Maybe there had been a slight translation problem with that last entry. I decided to stick with Humphrey's choice: another order of Peking Duck.

After spending a fine lunchtime with my new room-mate, we took a stroll around the block for more car spotting.

That night as we were getting ready for bed Hum-phrey needed to repack his bags. His backpack was the kind that opened at the top, which meant he had to remove all the contents to retrieve something at the bottom. It appeared he had packed every single item in a separate plastic bag, the kind that crinkled noisily when he stuffed his possessions back inside—as though he were wadding up Cellophane

Skrunch-skreech-skrinkle-skreech-skrunch.

I, too, pack my clothes in a couple of large plastic bags before stashing everything into my canvas backpack, especially if I plan to travel where rain is expected. But Humphrey was going to the extreme.

Skrunch-skreech-skrinkle-skreech-skrunch.

This went on for an hour, making sleep impossible. "Gee, Humphrey, how many plastic bags you got there?" I wondered out loud.

"Eighty-three," he proudly exclaimed. He was almost finished reloading his pack when he decided his toothbrush must be at the bottom. Out came eighty-three plastic bags. Since they were opaque and he couldn't see what was inside, he had to open every single one. The next morning Humphrey was thoughtful enough not to start unpacking until five a.m. Our tour wasn't scheduled to depart till midday.

He was also an early-morning-very-loud-gum-chewer. On the brighter side of things, his constant plastic-bag-skrunching-gum-chewing-distractions weren't as bad as his prolific flatulation.

A few days later we arrived at the Great Wall of China. Its 1,500-mile length stretches from the Yellow Sea in the east to a point deep in Gansu province in the west. Struggling up the wall's steep slopes and knowing that the structure meandered across rugged mountainous regions of China, it was easy to understand what a tremendous engineering feat it had been to build it so many centuries ago. The hordes of tourists climbing the wall with me that day provided great scale for my photographs as the late afternoon sun cast jagged shadows over the crenellated wall.

Weary from having carried all the photo gear I owned to the top, I returned to the bus just before sunset to discover that most of the other passengers on the tour were wearing an "I-CLIMBED-THE-GREAT-WALL" tee shirt.

Humphrey found me. His eyes sparkled as he proudly exclaimed, "There are 3,827 steps to the top of the Great Wall?"

He *was* a bit weird.

Humphrey loved to watch American cartoons on early morning television—though they were all dubbed into Chinese, which didn't seem to bother him very much. The volume was always turned *way* up because he was hard of hearing. After the third day of the trip, the screeching Chinese cartoon characters were about to drive me crazy. One night when Humphrey was taking a shower, I unplugged the cable connection to the television. At six a.m. the next morning he zapped on the TV with the remote control, which he always kept next to his pillow. Nothing but static, garbled Chinese and fuzzy pictures. But Humphrey was undaunted. He turned the volume up; he was having fun trying to figure out what the cartoon characters were saying. He'd probably already seen those same cartoons back home dozens of times.

After an hour of high-volume static, I couldn't stand it any more and started fumbling around the back of the television. "Humphrey, it looks as though the cable has come unplugged." I figured it would be far less disturbing to get the voice and picture back on.

Later that day our group climbed the highest hill in the Wolong Panda Reserve with the hope of glimpsing a wild panda or two. We had trudged over loose boulders and sliding scree, then snaked through a black tunnel chiseled through an almost impenetrable rock face. A subterranean spring gushed down on us. Trying to shield my cameras from the deluge, I slipped in the mud, smearing my trousers in slime and yuck.

At the top we stopped for a picnic lunch. Humphrey began reminiscing about his childhood days. "You know," he said, "when I was in the fifth grade, my history teacher's auto license plate number was YEB 732. My dad's was LQM 934 and my grandfather's was CBA 347."

(Honest, this really happened.)

We all had a great laugh and toasted Humphrey's brilliant memory. After an hour we packed our things and headed down the mountain, but the wild pandas must have heard us coming and went playing hide-and-seek.

At the bottom, Humphrey glanced up with a startled look on his face, then he apologized. He'd made a mistake. "My grandfather's license plate number wasn't CBA 347. It was CBA 743!"

A couple of days later our group trekked to a traditional Hmong thatched-roof village in the southern subtropical reaches of the Yunnan Province near the Burma, Laos and Vietnamese borders—an area populated by millions of non-Han Chinese ethnic tribal minorities. The inhabitants here form part of what the Chinese government refers to as the Autonomous

Minorities, though as with Tibet, their freedoms are restricted to the point of not really being all that "autonomous" anymore. Nevertheless, the local people have in large part maintained the distinctive influences of the dress, language and cultural mores of their southern neighbors, the hill-tribe peoples of Thailand, for example, who enjoy far more freedoms.

Our guide posed a curious question to our group: What did we think the bamboo turrets on the corner of each living compound were used for?

They appeared to be lookout posts for armed guards, who from that height could fend off hostile intruders. But our guide explained that these were peaceful people and had been for endless generations. For the life of us, none in our group could guess what these turrets were used for. And then we were told.

Each night a young unmarried girl of the family would position herself high in the turret to be serenaded by unmarried teenaged boys. And then, each night she would choose a partner for the evening. The object was for the young girl to become pregnant long before she got married. It was important to be educated in the arts of lovemaking, childbirth and child rearing prior to committing herself to a long-term relationship with a future husband. By the time the child would turn two or three years old the girl would have gained all the necessary experience to help provide a happy home atmosphere to raise her future family. Nuptial ceremonies were later conducted through an arranged marriage, the husband chosen by village elders.

Our guide explained that there were never any sexual crimes committed in this tribal society. My guess is there weren't any pent-up sexual frustrations either.

On the minibus ride back to our hotel that evening, Humphrey informed me that he'd counted a hundred and forty-seven bamboo turrets in the village.

On the last day of our trip, he was acting like an over-thrilled kid when he returned from a walk around town. Under his arm was a huge plastic bag with something large and round inside. "Guess what I found?" he proudly exclaimed.

Stretching my imagination, I said facetiously, "A giant hubcap!"

Humphrey looked astonished. "How did you know?"

I laughed my head off, knowing I'd never take another group tour as long as I lived.

15 TURKEY

Dozens of monumental phallic shapes surrounded me—those wild, eroded rock formations of
Cappadocia, which seem to capture the prurient fringes
of everyone's imagination.

I was in central Turkey getting ready to board a
hot-air balloon for a better view of what my guidebook
jokingly called this region of the Turkish landscape: Big
Willie Valley.

The formations reminded me of Bryce Canyon
National Park in Utah, except the erotically sculpted
formations of Cappadocia are far more distinctive.
Over the centuries a thick layer of volcanic tufa eroded
into gigantic phallic shafts or "chimneys" as they are
sometimes referred to in more modest guidebooks.
Hundreds of these towers proudly rise fifty or a hundred feet into the air. These structures of nature have
profiles that strikingly resemble certain aspects of the
aroused male Homo sapien anatomy—complete with
circumcision. (You won't question this observation
after seeing my photo on page 73.)

These formations must be seen to be believed.

I assisted the pilot in dragging the huge bag contain-
ing the balloon from his truck. We tugged and strained
to help wrench its massive bulk free of the bag. Yanking and stretching, we unfurled the balloon over the

flat terrain, first making sure we had removed sharp-pointed rocks from the area so that the fabric wouldn't be perforated. The pilot cranked up a gasoline-powered fan to pump air into the throat of the balloon. After a few minutes it lay half-inflated on the ground like a giant circus tent. I climbed inside the vast interior with a fisheye lens attached to my camera in an effort to capture an offbeat photo perspective. Enveloped by the balloon's multi-colored, herringbone stripes, it felt as though I were a tiny ant trapped inside a huge psyche-delic kaleidoscope.

Blistering flames blew toward me when the pilot blasted the propane burner to inject the balloon with heat so that it would begin to rise. The fiery outburst from the throat of the balloon conjured up visions in my mind of an angry dragon bellowing at its cave entrance.

The balloon began to lift underneath my feet.

The pilot waved for me to quickly finish shooting and get out of there as the dragon roared again, caus-ing the entire interior to light up as though a bomb had been detonated. In between two of those inflamed outbursts I dashed from the voluminous cavern, then crouched to climb into the wicker gondola lying on its side as the pilot busied himself getting the cables and propane hoses arranged. He provoked that propane burner into another snarl with several more bursts. The gondola began to right itself as the balloon became fully inflated. One more fiery discharge and our ascension had begun.

Then it became exceptionally quite as we floated along with the wind.

GLEN ALLISON

Between propane bursts, we drifted in solitude deeper and deeper into Big Willie Valley. Judging from the enormous scale of those phallic wonders, Mother Nature must have gone all out when she crafted them. We glided between shafts that were even taller than the height at which we flew.

An hour later our ride was over and we began our descent. From about twenty feet above the terrain the pilot finally coaxed the dragon to sleep by shutting down the propane burners. Then he pulled a special ripcord that opened a Velcro zipper across the top of the balloon. Hot air rushed out, sending us plummeting back to earth.

Before takeoff, the pilot had informed me that if his timing was right and there was no wind, when we landed the balloon would simply collapse and the gondola would touch down gently to earth. I could step out and my $200 balloon ride would be over. But the wind was strong that day, causing the rapidly deflating balloon to be dragged along sideways at least five hundred feet across rocky terrain, the gondola bouncing along on its side, my cameras banging against the wicker basket and me.

Luckily, I climbed out unscathed.

Now that I'd seen all those Big Willies from the air, I decided to trek through these natural wonders for photographs from a much lower perspective. Motivated by some primeval masculine urge, I found myself driven to shoot my own portrait with these phallic masterpieces framed in the background for posterity—and perspective. Then the idea just happened to occur to me that I might never have such a tempting opportunity again to align my profile with that of my surroundings in the perfect picture.

So I plopped myself on the ground—my legs spread to the wind—and I proceeded to frame one of those magnificent Willies as though it were part of my own anatomy.

16 TIBET

Despite the harsh reality of the 1959 Chinese takeover in Tibet and the havoc wreaked upon the Tibetan populace during the ensuing years, there remains embedded within the spiritual fabric of the people a perseverance that's both exhilarating and refreshing.

I hoped to capture their spirit on film.

My planned route of entry to the "Roof of the World" was across the Himalayas from Kathmandu to Lhasa, an overland trip that would cover almost six hundred miles of spectacular scenery through exquisite mountain valleys and over breathtaking 17,000-foot-high passes where the air would barely be breathable.

The tallest peaks in the world would surround me.

Though resplendent, the Tibetan landscape can be harsh in winter—the terrain is isolated, barren and bitterly cold. It wasn't an easy trip. There were washed-out roads to traverse and snow avalanches that had to climbed over hand and foot. The gale-force winds in the mountain passes were so strong I could hardly stand up, and the air was so meager it left me gasping, which ultimately led me to experience a terrible case of altitude sickness with extreme dizziness, nausea and dehydration. I thought I was about to die.

People have indeed been known to slip into a coma

and die before they could be taken down to lower altitudes. If a severe case of altitude sickness sets in, you must descend—fast—whether by porter, horse, yak or helicopter.

I had joined a half-dozen rather stalwart individuals to form a small tour group. Our plan was to traverse the Himalayas in four-wheel-drive vehicles, which would meet us on the Chinese side of the border. In Kathmandu we boarded our transportation and headed up the foothills of the Himalayas. At the last Nepalese border post, Kodari, we spent our first night at a rustic guesthouse. The next morning we boarded a cattle truck, which took us eleven kilometers up to the Chinese border-guard station at Zhangmu, through which we would enter Tibet. It was necessary to ride standing up in the bed of a cattle truck for several miles since there were no other vehicles sturdy enough to climb the steeply twisting narrow dirt road. Our backpacks were securely lashed to stakes along the side of the truck. Looking over the edge of the road was enough to give me vertigo. My knuckles turned white with the tight grip of my fingers on the handrail.

At the Chinese border our four-wheel-drive vehicles were nowhere to be seen. They'd been trapped by avalanches and were waiting in the next village for us, we were told. Our group must prepare to hike several miles up the slopes of the Himalayas. The winter had been long. There were tons of new snow and the likely possibility of more avalanches. We must be careful. Road crews had been sent out, we were informed, but phone lines were down, so there hadn't been communication for days with the villages along our proposed route.

We warmed ourselves with hot tea at a nearby restaurant and rallied confidence that another avalanche wouldn't bury us. We had to move fast not to be trapped by nightfall. Porters would carry our backpacks.

We were warned not to make too much noise negotiating the mountain passes. Noise could cause avalanches. My hands and feet were already freezing.

It was an arduous trek up the Himalayas. The passes were narrow; the road was steep. Under a charcoal sky, snowflakes fluttered through the drab afternoon light. At the bottom of the gorge below us, a turgid river pitched and churned over large chunks of ice. Tons of loosely packed snow loomed above us. With cupped hands shielding my face, I protected myself from a sudden gust of chilling wind. Wiping the snow from my goggles, I checked my watch. We'd trekked for three hours up the narrow road, forging a path through waist-high snowdrifts.

Another icy blast of wind whipped through the pass.

Around the next bend we had our first glimpse of a massive avalanche that straddled the road. Traversing this ominous pile of snow appeared impossible . . . and extremely dangerous. If we couldn't negotiate our way up and over this obstacle, there would be no alternative but to turn back.

Another avalanche could easily trap us. Most likely there wouldn't be a rescue. We had no radios to call for help. The visibility was too bad for helicopters to fly. If we became stranded, we'd probably die.

The piercing cold stung my cheeks.

The terrain was steep; the snow above looked unstable. We moved forward slowly, quietly. An avalanche now might mean our imminent burial. We made our way to the huge pile of snow that had engulfed the road in front of us. With the toe of my hiking boot I cautiously tested the edge of the avalanche. The snow was soft. When the wind whistled a fearful warning, I stepped back to find a more sure-footed stance. We'd probably be swallowed alive if we tried to plow our way across this perilous roadblock.

A stinging Arctic wind swept up the gorge, blasting more freezing sleet in our faces. I compacted the ice with each step forward to see if the avalanche would hold my weight, but I was buried in snow up to my waist. Inching along, we tightly gripped each other's wrists for support. I could almost hear the pulsating hearts. Twenty breathless minutes later, we'd clawed our way to the other side of the avalanche.

The road was icy and slippery; anyone tumbling over the edge would probably freeze to death in the river of ice below. Eventually we made it to the village of Tingri.

The town was packed with stranded travelers. Fortunately our hotel had saved us a large dorm room that we'd all have to share. It was a relief to see our two Land Rovers parked outside.

Wandering through the narrow streets of Tingri the next morning, I photographed the rustic faces of the nomadic mountain herders. (See my photo on page 79.) Their crooked teeth and leathery skin and narrow, laughing eyes were as intriguing as the traditional Tibetan architecture surrounding me. The people's faces were filled with calm dignity and the character of the harsh environment and the high-altitude living.

The men wore elaborate brocade hats with rabbit fur earflaps; the women had bands of red yarn and turquoise jewelry tied in their hair.

Three days later we were in the Tibetan capitol, Lhasa.

I awoke before daybreak to a chill wind. That day I wandered the streets for hours and visited the most revered Tibetan temple, Jokhang, which is located in the heart of the city. It was built more than fourteen hundred years ago but was almost destroyed when it was shelled and ransacked by Chinese Red Guards during the Cultural Revolution of the 1960s. For a number of years they used it as a pigsty.

Today endless lines of devotees pay homage here. The paving stones in the courtyard have been polished smooth by the prostration of immeasurable numbers of pilgrims over the centuries.

Late in the afternoon I climbed to the top of a hill just west of the Potala Palace. It had been the home of each successive Dalai Lama, the spiritual center of the Buddhist kingdom of Tibet—Shangri-La, the Land of the Snow Leopard.

The Potala rests on a huge mountain of granite that towers almost four hundred feet above the city. (Photo on pages 76-77.) Within its walls are a thousand deserted rooms—chapels with lavish altars, enameled incense burners, gilded shrines and elaborate tombs of past Dalai Lamas.

Over the centuries this grand palace served as a vibrant edifice to the hopes and aspirations of a proud people. Today it functions solely as a museum, a poignant reminder of the harsh challenges of life.

The sun cast deep, golden shadows across the jagged shapes of the palace walls. I watched countless worshipers making a holy, clockwise circumambulation of several miles, completely encircling their beloved city. I shivered in the chill wind. Every step of the way the pilgrims prostrated themselves flat on the ground, measuring mile after mile of the sacred route with the length of their prone bodies. It would probably take them days to complete even one trip around the city they loved. A city they would gladly die for, and for which many already had.

They continuously chanted and twirled tiny hand-held prayer wheels in one hand, holding a small picture of the Dalai Lama close to their chests in the other.

Their determination and faith struck me deeply.

The heritage of their city and their country had been virtually destroyed by the Chinese. Their spiritual leader was in exile. There appeared to be no chance that they would ever regain their country from the foreign invasion that had been meant to rob their souls of all hope. Yet, I could see the strength of their perseverance in their eyes. I watched as dozens of devotees prostrated their bodies far into the distance.

Virtually every cultural monument in Tibet, including more than six thousand monasteries and tons of sacred relics, were demolished or ransacked by the Chinese in their takeover. Three days after the Dalai Lama fled to India in 1959, tens of thousands of Tibetans were massacred when the Chinese troops quelled an immense popular uprising. Corpses had littered the streets of Lhasa for days.

The word "Lhasa" translates as "Ground of the

Gods." Nevertheless, the city has been treated shabbily by the Chinese ever since their forced takeover. Traditional Tibetan architecture has all but disappeared from the streetscape; the Chinese-built alternative constructions are all but aesthetic. And there's little hope that the former beauty of Lhasa will ever be restored.

Even at this moment the harsh hand of Chinese rule stands ready to crush demonstrations and protests, even if most of the troops are not seen. But they're not very far away, and they're poised for action at the first sign of unrest. Periodic revolts of the past few decades have been mercilessly suppressed. Since May of 2000 visiting tourists have been required to travel with a guide who is Chinese or at least Chinese-educated. Tibetan guides are no longer allowed. Trying to travel independently in the country, you could put locals you encounter at the risk of being "re-educated" just because they assisted you in providing directions, or perhaps by offering you a room and a meal. I visited Tibet in the mid-nineties, prior to these new rules. But today even hard-core veteran travelers obtain official guides so as not to endanger the lives or livelihood of locals who might offer assistance.

The world turned a blind eye four decades ago when the Chinese invaded Tibet. Today it might not appear that the country is still in a Chinese police state.

But it is.

17 TIMBUKTU

The noise was oppressive, the pollution was unbearable, the heat was searing. The unruly Harmattan winds were blowing in from the Sahara Desert, which lay just a few hundred kilometers to the north.

Dust and sand filled the air, all but obscuring the driver's vision as he daringly attempted to negotiate bumper-to-bumper congestion. Horns blared. It might have been faster for me to walk the streets of Bamako, Mali. At least my taxi driver spoke a bit of English, though with a deeply layered, nasal French accent. French is the official language in this North African, land-locked nation where thirty tribal languages are spoken. I had already concluded that finding my own way around Bamako—a city with street signs that appeared unintelligible—would get me nowhere fast. Obviously my taxi wasn't making much better progress.

Up ahead, I spotted an elegant African woman clad in a wild splash of color that caught my eye. She was crisscrossing between lanes of immobile vehicles, most of them dinked and kinked and in much need of new paint or body repairs, and she was heading my way. Her high cheekbones and chiseled-cut features were striking.

Sometimes I can't resist snapping discreet photos of local residents, especially if they're wrapped in pictur-

GLEN ALLISON

esque garb. Naturally that leaves me without permission to take their picture in the first place, and most definitely it leaves me without a model release . . . which would be required by stock photo libraries if they accepted those images and licensed them for publication. I know that in some cultures the locals feel that taking photographs of them is stealing their souls. I must respect that. I've got enough to worry about just keeping my own soul in tact.

Usually I try to get releases after the fact if I've succeeded in capturing a phenomenal picture using my strategies of stealth. Many photo agencies refuse to accept images without releases, no matter what the future use might be. Sales for advertising (the biggest money earner) would be out of the question sans release, without assuming extreme liability risks—risks usually dumped back into the photographer's lap by the agency's onerous contract, which he or she had signed. One never knows when a Third World native might have an uncle practicing law in New York City.

Clipped to my belt was a tiny Nikon 28Ti pocket camera. It's so small it might pass for a cheapy point-n-shoot model, but in reality it's a top-of-the-line unit with an incredibly sharp lens, a camera that costs a thousand dollars. I frequently put it to use when I don't want to draw attention from petty thieves, times when I prefer to look more like a tourist and less like a professional photographer carrying expensive gear.

As the African lady neared, I quickly slipped the Nikon from its pouch at my waist, flipped the switch to pop out the lens, palmed the camera in my hand and dropped my arm out the window ready to snap a photo of her when she walked by. I've learned to shoot surreptitiously "from the hip" in such situations without needing to look through the viewfinder to frame the picture.

Click! A perfect composition, I already knew.

The woman's face was filled with strength and dignity. She was incredibly beautiful. And I should have captured the perfect candid composition without her ever having known it. Except the damn flash had fired. Crap! In the rush of the moment I'd forgotten to turn the switch off.

The woman screamed.

We were jammed between cars stopped at a traffic light and there wasn't any escape for our taxi. Faster than the flash of the camera, a street cop appeared from out of nowhere. He yanked open the car's door and attempted to drag me outside. But I braced my foot against the door frame and refused to budge. My driver looked scared. I was resolute—if not totally crazed. The cop was trying to wrench the camera from my tightly clutched fist as I vehemently fought back. Now that I'd bungled my clandestine attempt at immortalizing the beautiful woman's image on film and was experiencing this nightmare as a result, she didn't look so beautiful any more. Her face tightened with anger. She kept shouting in her native tongue utterances that definitely sounded like harsh words—probably in the language of Bambara or Kalongo or Masasi or Somono or Malinké or Songhay or Tamasheg. In the heat of the confusion and of the day I couldn't make out the exact dialect.

My bravado rapidly diminished and I concluded that the picture wasn't worth facing a firing squad. By now I'd probably already blown my chance of getting a model release from the woman anyway. My Nikon was too expensive to lose just because of intimidation or duress. So I snapped open the back, ripped out a 36-exposure strip of film and flung it toward the hostile policeman. By then the traffic light had changed and my driver stomped his foot on the gas pedal. I ducked below the seat just in case bullets were fired as we sped away from the scene.

This was my first day in Mali.

A few days latter I traveled north to Djenné, arriving just before sunset. After checking into a hotel I strolled through winding alleys and crooked streets, eventually finding my way to the central square, dominated on one side by the famous Djenné Mosque—the largest mud structure in the world, an architectural feat that defines classic Sudanese primitive architecture. The lowering sun cast mysterious shadows across the mosque's three towering minarets, whose façades are perforated with wooden posts that not only create a unique design but also serve as scaffolding for repairs after the rare, though sometimes heavy seasonal rains, which can cause the mud walls to dissolve.

The steps up to the mosque symbolize the transition from the world of the irreverent to that of the divine. The interior is said to be impressive. An array of ninety pillars supports the heavy wooden roof. But infidels are no longer allowed inside. Only Muslim believers. It seems that a few years ago a French fashion photographer used the interior as a surreal setting for his skimpily dressed models posed in provocative stance. Staunch Muslim clerics then changed the entrance rules.

The morning after my arrival, I set out to capture

the quintessential photo of Djenné. For a hundred bucks (an obvious rip-off considering local monetary standards) I arranged to have a dozen brilliantly out-fitted, and already model-released, African ladies pose in casual conversation in front of the famous mud mosque.

But then a problem ensued. Five or six mischievous young boys on bicycles kept riding across the frame of my viewfinder just behind the row of chattering women.

I threatened to not pay the hundred dollars to the street hustler who'd arranged for the ladies to be there if he didn't get rid of the kids who were ruining my picture. The man grabbed a huge stick and proceeded to club the itinerant boys. When I saw the impending harm to the kids and the malevolent intent in the tout's eyes, I completely freaked out. No picture was worth human beings getting hurt. I hurriedly dashed between club and children, demanding he stop. The scene was beyond anything I could ever have imagined. The tout's greed for money had instantly brought violence to the fore. I was determined to defuse the situation. The kids sensed I meant business and they quickly disappeared. The tout ceased and desisted. I went back to my picture, though it was difficult to work knowing what had almost happened. By the time the shooting session was finished, my pulse rate had simmered down. I paid the man the hundred bucks, knowing I'd never do business with the likes of him again. Somehow I brought smiles to the women's faces. (See my photo, pages 80-81.)

Mali is the home of fabled Timbuktu.

But before I journeyed there, I first embarked on

a five-day trek across the African Sahel—a transitional zone lying just south of the Sahara, a region of semi-arid desert and thorny scrub brush. My goal: to photograph the Dogon mud villages, which have for centuries precariously clung to the 500-foot-high cliffs of the Bandiagara Escarpment. (Photo on pages 82-83.) Thirty years ago, back when I was studying architecture at UC Berkeley, I'd come across a book called *Architecture without Architects*. In it were phenomenal photographs of the Dogon villages laid out in a cityscape of modular shapes clutching the vertical cliff-side. I vowed I'd go see them in the future.

And now I was here.

By day I climbed the Bandiagara cliffs, photographing the conical thatched-roof mud huts, women grinding millet and men performing the traditional funeral dances. I played with the kids. By night I pitched my tent on the desert floor below.

During spring each year the turbulent, sand-laden Harmattan winds blow furiously, bringing the heat of the Sahara and turning the country into a dust bowl. The Sahara generates an estimated 300 million tons of dust and sand each year, and the fierce winds blanket much of this deluge across northern Africa. The skies become obscured. It's like photographing through a dense orange fog filter with gritty smudge on the glass surface.

On the first night at my campground I gathered four immense boulders, one to be placed in each corner of my tent in case the tent and I took flight during the night. Throughout the evening the wind howled in a frenetic tumult as if to assert its authority. This only added to the eerie presence of the majestic cliff dwellings rising above me in the dark and the dead people hanging up there in the caves.

The Dogons are animists.

Their history is based on a rather obscure oral tradition, but most scholars agree that they weren't the first inhabitants of these cliffs. A mysterious people of pygmy descent known as the Tellem—said to have magical powers—were their predecessors. The Tellem buried their dead in caves high above their cliff-hanging villages.

Dogons believe that when they die their soul leaves the body but it remains in the village for some time. Three separate funeral ceremonies must be performed before the dead can join the spiritual world of their ancestors. The first burial occurs immediately after death, and in many cliff villages the corpses are hoisted by ropes to their final abode high in the age-old burial caves of the Tellem. The Dogons believe, however, that the soul of the deceased remains in the family house for up to a year, thus providing the household ample time to properly mourn and—perhaps more important—to save up enough money for a proper burial celebration complete with large quantities of millet beer to be consumed by the celebrants. After much inebriation the deceased's soul is invited to leave the family, but it's believed these spirits reside somewhere in the village for at least another five years. At that time elaborately decorated, masked dancers (see my photo on pages 84-85) lead the departed souls out to the bush to rejoin their ancestors.

Lying in my tent alone with the Harmattan howling around me, I sure hoped none of those ancient souls decided to come inside with me to escape the turbulent winds of the night.

In Dogon lore it's believed that each soul is born in a state that simultaneously manifests both male and female aspects of sexuality. Neither predominates over the other until circumcision rites are performed. With the removal of the foreskin or clitoris—the physical expression of one's actual sex—the individual can then become male or female definitively. But the rejected half of one's spiritual sexuality is not destroyed by the mere act of circumcision. The Dogon believe that the excised clitoris transforms into a scorpion and that the foreskin becomes a lizard, thus enabling the male and female souls of each person to survive as twins in the animal world.

The most distinctive feature of Dogon villages is the square-shaped, thatched-roof granaries where the inhabitants store their millet and other personal belongings. Each granary has an elaborately carved wooden door depicting village life in bas-relief. Not many of these treasured relics are left. Unfortunately these artifacts have become the desire of souvenir-hungry tourists and unscrupulous art dealers across the globe.

Perhaps even more unusual are the circular structures on the outskirts of each village known as *maison des femmes* or menstruation houses. As in many primitive societies Dogon women are considered to be impure during their menstrual cycle and as such they are banished to these outlying domains. Many of the structures are decorated with elaborate mud carvings of men and women with huge sexual organs. Many of these displays are even embellished with real pubic hair.

On the last day of my Dogon trek I came across a man selling hand-carved wooden figures. My guide had already explained the significance about the male/female scenario of Dogon ritual. These sculptures of nude Dogon villagers were male on one side and female on the other—the perfect symbolic union. The going price of the artefacts was the equivalent of about ten U.S. dollars; the Dogons don't bargain. I was running low on domestic currency and the man wouldn't accept U.S. bills. He wanted local money in CFAs or at least French francs, neither of which I had enough. Not to worry. The man asked my guide when he'd next be passing through the area, and the guide explained that it might be three or four months hence. No problem. I was welcome to take the sculpture and pay the guide the ten bucks in local currency at the end of my trek. The seller would trust that he'd get his payment some time in the future. Such honesty was extremely heartwarming to my soul. I later learned that the Dogons truly believe that if they cheat each other they surely will die. How come the Western world hasn't realized this? At the end of my trip I gladly paid my guide the ten dollars; I wasn't ready to die yet.

Then I boarded a small plane for the short flight to the southern edge of the Sahara and the isolated, though legendary city of Timbuktu, long regarded as perhaps the most remote and inaccessible place on the planet.

I stepped from the tiny plane onto the deserted runway. A sea of billowing sand peppered my face, the Harmattan wind now more vehement than ever.

All I saw was sand swirling in every direction, a few mud houses, a mud mosque or two. No water. Nothing green. The effects, I imagined, of a virtual absence of rain for perhaps the last eon. The torturous heat seemed like it might melt my skin. There was no possibility for anything to grow here. As far as my eyes could see, everything was dry and bleak. There were almost no people. Not what I expected to find in the world's most fabled city, the cultural crossroads of the ancient Trans-Sahara caravan routes where endless streams of Tuareg nomads had for millennia guided their camels across the dessert—camels laden with treasures of gold and frankincense and myrrh.

Timbuktu is, quite literally, on the edge of the desert. The town isn't big. The few streets are disjointed and sandy. The sparse houses are of mud and are blandly designed. Though there's only one paved road, I soon discovered that the Internet is here.

In keeping with the myriad ways place names are spelled on maps and street signs in Mali, it didn't take long for me to realize that I was actually in Timbuktu or Timbuctoo or Tombouctou. But no matter how you spell it, this desolate place is unquestionably located in the middle of nowhere.

Finally I had arrived at the end of the earth.

18 FINAL COMMENTS

haven't told a personal story about each of the 131 countries and territories I visited during the past decade, but I can truly say I loved them all in some unique way. Many people ask which destination was my favorite. I simply reply, "The next one."

The world is an exquisite place, even though everywhere we look it's so easy to find anguish and heartache. Hatred and bigotry have a way of ruining everything. That's so sad. I'm convinced that we as global citizens must celebrate the differences amongst ourselves, otherwise how will there ever be peace on this earth?

I hope you have enjoyed our little trip—all three thousand one hundred and fifty-five nonstop days that it took me to complete it.

Of course, my journey isn't over yet.

I apologize if I might have poked some gentle fun at your culture or perhaps your favorite destination, for in reality I was trying to poke fun at my own narrow-minded viewpoints. Thanks for indulging me and for sharing some of the lessons I learned.

Traveling isn't always easy. Perhaps it's not important how long your trip might be or how far you might go. Even if my journey lasts only one day and only takes me to the next city, I know I must strive to create value in some little way. But so many times I've let opportunities slip past so quickly.

I'm determined to stop that.

No matter where we might travel, it's easy to find pain and suffering inflicted on innocent people. Surely we ordinary citizens can steer world leaders to create a safer and saner future. In the end, it's only the individual who can make change happen. We must choose hope. Let's discard violence. Let's manifest the awesome power of human imagination in finding ways to accomplish this task.

I'll try harder.

Quoting again from Dr. Daisaku Ikeda's *For the Sake of Peace*: "The time has come for the ordinary people, those who have been tossed about on the waves of war and violence in the twentieth century, to take the leading role in history. They must take the initiative in constructing a new framework for symbiosis. By linking hands in an alliance that transcends national borders, the people can realize a world without war and make our third millennium an era of bright-hued hope."

As I mentioned in the first chapter, my goal is to forge a lifelong friendship with at least one person in every single country of the world. Before I leave this precious Earth, I will visit them all . . . many times.

Perhaps our paths will cross somewhere along the way. I hope so.

Bon voyage!

ABOUT THE AUTHOR

Glen Allison is a travel photographer and writer based in Los Angeles. He's had more than 50,000 travel images published worldwide. Last decade, roaming the globe with not much more in his backpack than a few changes of clothes, a laptop computer and a camera, he embarked on a nonstop eight-year journey, maintaining no permanent residence while he photographed 131 countries and territories. Glen has a degree in architecture from UC Berkeley. He is a founder of the Stock Artists Alliance photographer advocacy group and holds a leadership position in the Soka Gakkai International world peace organization—roles that continue to hone his understanding of human nature. He has also penned an adventure/love story novel *The Journey from Kamakura*.

http://www.GlenAllison.com
http://www.PenisGourds.com
http://www.JourneyFromKamakura.com

Comments are invited at the e-mail address:

gourds@TenWorldPress.com

Glen's photographs can be viewed on the Internet by entering his name in the search engines at the following web sites:

http://www.gettyimages.com
http://www.alamy.com
http://www.mira.com
http://www.workbookstock.com
http://www.agefotostock.com

TENWORLDPRESS